FIVE CARD MAJOR BIDDING
IN CONTRACT BRIDGE

FIVE CARD MAJOR BIDDING
IN CONTRACT BRIDGE

Harold Feldheim

Published by
Devyn Press
Louisville, Kentucky

DEDICATION

To Myrna and Bob Lurie who spent countless hours finding fourteen card hands;

To Simon Rich who found great amusement correcting my syntax;

To my devil's advocate, the Mighty McAdoo;

To Shirley and Harry Silverman, for their advice, encouragement and perseverance;

And to Sue, my wife, my love, and preserver of my sanity through all of this.

Devyn Press, Inc.
3600 Chamberlain Lane, Suite 230
Louisville, KY 40241
1-800-274-2221

CONTENTS

FOREWORD

A majority of the bridge players in the United States and Canada use a five card major bidding system. In its simplest form it is easy to learn and produces good results, even for the casual player.

But why do the experts also use this system? Because they also find that it has the twin virtues of simplicity and accuracy.

However, the expert player wants perfection; he hopes to be in the correct contract on every hand. To accomplish this, he has refined the basic five card major structure to include conventions such as the negative double, the forcing notrump and new minor forcing. As each of these is added, accuracy increases.

This book explains the basic five card major approach, plus all the refinements that can be added to it. Further, it shows their *raison d'etre* so that the reader can place them firmly into an integrated bidding system.

Never forget that bidding accuracy depends on partnership understanding. When a bad result occurs, write down the hand and refer back to the relevant section in the book to see where you went wrong. Recriminations at the table lead to bad games; constructive discussion produces winners. May all your games be winning ones!

—Shirley Silverman

EDITOR'S NOTE

It has been a pleasure to edit another of Harold Feldheim's creations. The strain on the brain (and the throat) as we argued the fine points of bidding were amply repaid by the winning advice contained in the final product.

—Thomas McAdoo Smith

PREFACE

Do you play "four card majors"? Do you play "five card majors"? Do you THINK you play "five card majors"? If the answer to any of these questions is yes, then you will find much of interest and value in this book.

If you already play five card majors, we will try to help you develop a more cohesive bidding structure. If you play four card majors, this book will show how, with a few simple adjustments, you can gain increased bidding ease and accuracy.

We assume that the reader has a basic knowledge of Standard American bidding, including the Stayman and Blackwood conventions, and that he uses the standard 4-3-2-1 point count with distributional adjustments. Some bids will remain in your system, but a few of the old dogs in your kennel will be taught new bidding tricks.

We begin with a discussion of major suit openings and the development of the auction that follows and then move on to minor suit auctions and the thorny problems that arise. The sections on conventions and treatments will be of special interest to those readers whose use of five card major openings is limited to grafts onto an otherwise Standard American approach.

While many readers will doubtless choose to adopt only some of the conventions and treatments in this book, we urge you to study all of them carefully. They comprise a cohesive bidding system as opposed to a random assortment of conventions and treatments. If your memory will not allow you to add all the bids at once, try adding them one at a time. When you are comfortable with one, add another. The increased accuracy in bidding will spur you on to an eventual use of the entire bidding structure.

INTRODUCTION

Before discussing the whys and wherefores of five card majors, let's take a brief look at the bridge world of the 1940's. The four card major structure used then had a simplicity which negated the need for many conventions. Bid suits were at least four cards in length and non-competitive auctions usually (though not always) proceeded smoothly.

However, there was a slow though steady trend towards opening only five card majors until today the vast majority of experts play a five card major system: Eastern or Western Scientific, Precision, Kaplan-Sheinwold or Roth-Stone.

To play five card majors, there is a necessity to occasionally open the bidding with a three card minor and to employ a few new conventions. "Why bother?" you may ask. Simple — to attain a level of bidding accuracy that is not available within a four card major structure.

Assume you hold:

♠ 10 3 2   ♡ A 4   ◇ K J 10 4   ♣ 9 8 7 6

and partner opens with one spade. A five card majorite bids two spades in a flash, confident of an eight card fit and a potential ruffing value in hearts. The four card majorite **might** raise to two spades or he **might** bid one notrump. Either call could be right — or wrong.

A full analysis of the virtues of "fours" versus "fives" is beyond the scope of this book, but we have no doubt that the reader can construct many examples of the value of knowing for sure that partner holds at least five cards in the suit when he opens hearts or spades.

Use of the "forcing notrump" and "negative double" conventions are vital to gain maximum effect from a five card major system. These are quite simple and are fully explained later in the book.

The necessity to open the bidding with a three card minor need not cause alarm. Both partners will be aware of this possibility and should have no problem sidestepping any auction accident.

One more word. Since bridge players have different styles, we've included a couple of optional treatments. Study them and try them out. Even if you choose the more standard approach, you will have a useful understanding should these bids appear as part of your opponents' repertoire.

THE FIVE CARD MAJOR OPENING

As implied by the title, the opening bidder must hold at least five cards in the named suit to open with one heart or one spade, plus opening bid values. When considering how to open the bidding, the following is the priority of choice (provided the hand does not qualify for a notrump or preemptive opening bid):

1. A five card major or longer;
2. A four card minor or longer;
3. A three card minor.

Let's look at some hands and construct a few simple rules.

(1) ♠ J 5 4 3 2   ♡ A 4   ◇ A K Q 5 4   ♣ 10

One spade. Open with a five card major despite the strength of the diamond suit. With five-five, open the bidding with the higher ranking suit.

(2) ♠ A K 5 4 3   ♡ Q   ◇ J 3   ♣ K J 10 4 2

This is the only exception to #1. With five clubs and five spades, open with one club, planning to bid and rebid the spade suit.*

(3) ♠ 5 4 2   ♡ A K Q 5   ◇ Q 9 8 7   ♣ K 4

One diamond. Since you may not open one heart without five hearts, open with your four card minor.

(4) ♠ A K J 9   ♡ 5 4 3   ◇ Q 5 4   ♣ A 10 8

One club. Since you hold neither a five card major nor a four card minor, you must open with a three card minor. **RULE:** When you hold three cards in each minor, open with the stronger suit. If the suits are approximately of equal strength, open with one club.

(5) ♠ A K 10 5   ♡ Q J 3   ◇ A K 5   ♣ 10 9 3

One notrump. Don't lose track of simple bidding. With a flat hand and 16 to 18 points, open one notrump.

---

*Some experts advocate a spade opening, but this often leads to awkward bidding sequences.

(6) ♠ K J 10 3   ♡ Q J 5 4   ◊ 10 5 4   ♣ A K

One diamond. With no five card major and no four card minor, open your longer minor regardless of suit quality. Never open with a two card suit, no matter how good it is.

(7) ♠ 10 6 5 4 2   ♡ A K Q 5 3   ◊ K 4   ♣ 7

One spade. With equal distribution (at least 5-5) in the majors, open one spade.

(8) ♠ A K J   ♡ Q 4   ◊ J 5 4 3   ♣ K 5 4 3

One diamond. With four cards in each minor, open with one diamond.

(9) ♠ A J 9   ♡ Q 4 3   ◊ 5 4 3 2   ♣ A Q J

One diamond. With four diamonds and three clubs, open one diamond, despite any difference in strength.

Summary of Opening Bids

In order of preference:
    1. A five card major or longer;
    2. A four card minor or longer;
    3. A three card minor.

With two five card suits, open the bidding in the higher ranking suit. The only exception to this rule is a holding of five clubs and five spades.

With four clubs and four diamonds (and no five card major), open the bidding with one diamond.

With three clubs and three diamonds (and no five card major), open the bidding with the better three card minor.

If it is necessary to open with a short minor, open the three card suit, regardless of high card holding. Never open with the doubleton, no matter how strong.

* * *

The first section of this book will deal with responder's bids in support of opener's five card major opening bid. From there we will explore other sequences. As mentioned earlier, there are a few conventions to learn. The small effort will be rewarded by an accurate bidding structure with a minimum of guesswork and a maximum of successful contracts.

RAISING PARTNER'S MAJOR SUIT OPENING BID

Whenever responder holds three or more trumps opposite partner's major suit opening bid, there is a known holding of at least eight trumps between the two hands. For this reason, it is normally advantageous to confirm a trump fit by immediately raising partner's suit.

Raises are directly related to the high card strength and texture of responder's hand and can be roughly divided into four categories:

1. The non invitational raise, five to ten points.

2. The invitational (limit) raise, approximately ten to twelve points.

3. The game forcing raise, approximately eleven or more points.

4. The preemptive raise to game, based on distribution.

This must necessarily be a rough division because a ten point hand might be considered a simple raise or worthy of a game try. Similarly, an eleven point hand can be treated as a game try or a game force. These problems are matters of judgment. As we discuss each category, the guiding principles will be illustrated as an aid to close decisions. (All illustrations in these sections assume no interference bidding by the opponents.)

THE NON INVITATIONAL RAISE

One Heart — Two Hearts / One Spade — Two Spades

A simple raise to the two level indicates a below average hand (five to ten points) with three or more trumps and is not particularly forward-going. Opener should pass if his bid is in the minimum range but he can bid again if he holds extra values. He can invite game with extra values (16 to 18 points) or leap directly to game with a better hand.

What action should you take after partner opens the bidding with a major suit and right hand opponent passes, if you hold each of the following hands?

(1) ♠ A Q 5 4   ♡ J 10 3 2   ◊ J 7   ♣ 4 3 2

A classic raise to the two level. This is a better than average single raise in either major, but with only eight high card points, game is unlikely unless the opener has a very good hand.

(2) ♠ A Q 7   ♡ Q 5 4 3   ◊ J 8 7 4   ♣ 7 2

Again, a simple raise is the correct response in either major, but this is a closer decision than Hand (1). With nine high card points and a doubleton club, we count ten playing points. Nevertheless, a conservative simple raise is appropriate because of the poor quality of the outside points. Partner needs extra values for game to have a reasonable chance. Close decisions often are based on high card point quality. One ace is better than two queens; jacks are always questionable assets. (This hand is more valuable after a one heart opening, but still not worth more than a minimum raise.)

(3) ♠ Q 8 4   ♡ 10 9 4 3   ◊ Q 5 4 2   ♣ 8 4

Bidding with this hand is almost guaranteed to achieve a minus score! If partner holds minimum values, he is unlikely to make his contract; if he holds extra values, he will probably press on to an unsafe level. The proper technique is to pass. Only after the opponents balance or if partner shows signs of life, should you support partner's major. Conveying information about weakness is just as important as conveying information about strength.

(4) ♠ K J 10 8 ♡ A J 5 3 ◇ 7 ♣ 8 7 6 5

This hand is far too strong for a simple raise. With nine high card points plus three distributional points, the correct action is either an invitational or game forcing bid. How we bid this hand will be covered later in this chapter, but it is important to understand that raising to two of partner's major would be a gross underbid. Whenever game is a real possibility even opposite a minimum opening, the simple raise is inappropriate.

(5) ♠ J 5 3 ♡ 2 ◇ A 8 7 6 4 2 ♣ J 10 9
(Partner opens one spade.)

Again, a classic raise to the two level. This is a better than average two spade raise but game is unlikely unless opener has a very good hand.

Rebids By Opener

After the auction one of a major—two of a major, opener passes with minimum values and bids further with extra values. If opener holds a huge hand, such as

♠ A 3 2 ♡ A Q 10 9 7 ◇ A K 7 ♣ K 2

and partner responds two hearts to his one heart opening, there is no problem; he leaps directly to a game. The two heart response gives sufficient information for opener to know that the combined partnership holdings are sufficient for game but not enough for slam.

Problems arise when partner's raise to the two level provides insufficient information. Let's take the same hand, minus the ace of spades:

♠ 4 3 2 ♡ A Q 10 9 7 ◇ A K 7 ♣ K 2

After the auction one heart — two hearts, opener's hand evaluates to approximately 18 points: 16 high card points, one point for distribution, and one point for length in a supported suit. He wishes to investigate the possibility of game, but how should he do it?

In the "good old days," invitational sequences would be one heart — two hearts — three hearts, asking responder to pass with a minimum and bid game with a maximum. Of course, this tells responder nothing beyond the fact that opener holds extra values. During the 1940's, theoreticians realized that the important criterion was not whether responder held maximum values but rather the location of responder's values.

To assist responder's decision-making process, the modern player inaugurates a "game try" by bidding a new suit. A new suit bid can have either of two meanings depending on partnership agreement. It is vital to discuss this with your partner.

(a) "Short suit" game try — usually a singleton or void.

(b) "Help suit" game try — requesting partner's help in the suit.

The short suit game try is an excellent way to convey information to responder. Developed by Edgar Kaplan and Alfred Sheinwold as part of their system, this bid is designed to make responder aware of what may be a useless holding. As an example, you hold:

♠ J 5 3   ♡ K J 7 4   ◇ K 3   ♣ 8 7 4 3

After the auction one spade — two spades, suppose partner tries for game by bidding three hearts, showing heart shortness. Despite the maximal quality of your original spade raise, you decline partner's invitation by signing off with three spades. The value of the king and jack of hearts are considerably lessened by partner's probable singleton. Interchange the club and heart holdings:

♠ J 5 3   ♡ 8 7 4 3   ◇ K 3   ♣ K J 7 4

and now responder should accept the invitation by leaping directly to four spades. The king and jack of clubs are "working" cards, while the opponents' high cards in hearts will be ruffed away by partner. Opener's hand might look something like:

♠ A K 10 7 4   ♡ 10   ◇ A J 4 2   ♣ Q 10 2

The location of responder's high cards becomes the critical factor in determining game prospects. With heart honors, game is unlikely; with high clubs (or club shortness), game in spades becomes a fine contract.

Utilizing help suit game tries (the most common form of game invitation, by the way), opener would rebid three clubs on the above hand since that is where help is needed. With club honors or shortness in clubs, responder bids game.

Consider the following five situations. In each case, partner has raised your one spade opening to two spades.

(1) ♠ A Q J 8 7　♡ A K 3　◇ Q 5 4 3　♣ 2

With 16 high card points plus a singleton club, game is a distinct possibility but by no means certain. Playing short suit game tries, the correct bid is three clubs, asking partner to carry on to game if his values are outside the club suit. The help suit game try is three diamonds, asking partner to bid game with help in diamonds. (This "help" may be in the form of either high cards or ruffing values; a singleton or doubleton diamond would be very useful since you would be able to trump your losing diamonds in dummy.)

(2) ♠ J 7 5 4 3 2　♡ A K　◇ A K Q 7　♣ 2

A game try should be used only when partner's original raise does not supply sufficient information for you to make an intelligent decision. With this excellent hand, partner's raise is enough to leap directly and confidently to four spades.

(3) ♠ A K Q J 7　♡ Q 5 4　◇ J 10 7　♣ Q 2

As in the previous example, partner's raise conveys sufficient information for you to make an intelligent decision; this holding dictates a pass. While it is certainly possible to construct a responding hand that provides good chances for game, e.g.:

♠ 10 9 8 4　♡ 3 2　◇ A Q 9 8　♣ K 9 7

where the game depends only on a successful diamond finesse, on balance game is unlikely opposite most single raises. This hand offers the unwary player a distinct trap; he may "fall in love" with his excellent trump holding, overlooking the terrible quality of his side suits.

(4) ♠ K Q 10 9 7　♡ 4　◇ K 10 8 4　♣ A K 4

With 15 high card points plus a singleton heart, this hand is certainly worth a game try. A short suit game try dictates a rebid of three hearts while three diamonds would be a help suit game try, asking partner to make a decision based on his diamond holding. In either case, responder should have sufficient information to make an intelligent bid.

(5) ♠ K 10 9 7 4   ♡ A K J   ◇ A 10 9   ♣ Q 8

Despite the five card spade suit, it would not have been unreasonable to start the bidding on this hand with one notrump. Assuming that you opened with one spade, two notrump would be an appropriate game try, showing scattered values, an unprepossessing trump suit and a balanced hand. Responder has the options of passing, signing off in three spades, or bidding game in either notrump or spades. (This rare type of game try is utilized with 16 to 18 high card points and 5-3-3-2 distribution.) (A word to the wise reader: In many sections of this book you will be presented with alternative treatments. Please use whichever you and partner feel most comfortable with. *Be sure that you and partner agree.)*

THE LIMIT RAISE

Partner opens the bidding with one heart, right hand opponent passes and you hold:

♠ A 7   ♡ K 10 5 3   ◊ K 9 5 4   ♣ 4 3 2

With ten high card points, a potentially useful doubleton and four good trumps, the hand is clearly too strong for a simple two heart response, but it is too weak to insist on game; if partner holds minimum values, four hearts has little chance. Modern bidders solve this problem by treating a single jump in partner's suit as a highly invitational bid, stronger than a simple raise but showing less than game forcing values. A "limit raise" of three hearts would therefore be the correct response to partner's one heart opening with this hand. This asks partner to bid game with a sound opening bid, while giving him the option of passing with shaded values.*

The following examples should clarify some of the do's and don't's of limit raises:

(1) ♠ K 9 5 3   ♡ A 8 7 6   ◊ K 3 2   ♣ 5 4
     (Partner opens with one spade.)

This is the classic limit raise — a hand too strong for a simple raise but not quite strong enough for a forcing raise. A jump to three spades solves all problems. After partner's one spade opening you do not have sufficient data to make an intelligent decision. Your ace and two kings may be enough for game or even slam. Pass the decision to partner and see what he has to say.

---

*Those readers who are used to treating one heart — three hearts or one spade — three spades as a forcing sequence need not worry. An alternate bid for the strong hand will be presented later.

(2) ♠ Q J 8 5 2   ♡ Q 10 4   ◇ Q 3 2   ♣ Q 9
(Partner opens with one spade.)

Despite the fifth trump and nine high card points, this hand is worth only a two spade raise. Nine points is a borderline area between a simple raise and a limit raise. The doubleton club queen cannot be counted both for its distributional value and as a high card. Also, the hand contains no first or second round controls. To determine whether or not to be optimistic with a nine or ten count, check for control cards. An ace is generally more useful than two queens or a queen and two jacks. The more controls, the better the hand.

(3) ♠ 3 2   ♡ K 10 2   ◇ A Q 10 3   ♣ Q 5 4 2
(Partner opens with one heart.)

The limit raise should virtually guarantee four card trump support. (Later in this book, we will discuss the forcing notrump response which includes a sequence showing a limit raise with only three card trump support). However, for the time being, this hand certainly is worth an invitation to a heart game and, until you adopt forcing notrump responses, three hearts is an acceptable bid.

(4) ♠ 10   ♡ 10 5 4 3   ◇ A 9 8 7   ♣ A 8 7 6
(Partner opens with one heart.)

Despite holding only eight high card points, three points should be added for the singleton. A limit raise to three hearts is the correct action; a mere raise to two hearts would be cowardly. Partner will pass two hearts holding a hand such as:

♠ J 7 4   ♡ A K 9 8 7   ◇ K Q 3   ♣ 3 2

and, barring horrendous distribution, a contract of four hearts will almost certainly be a success. When conducting an auction, it is important to include distribution in your hand evaluation and bid accordingly.

(5) ♠ K 5 4 2   ♡ 3 2   ◇ 5 4   ♣ A K J 10 3
(Partner opens with one spade.)

A three spade response, showing limit raise values, is poor for two reasons. First, this hand is a bit too strong — with eleven high card points and two doubletons, you have game forcing values in support of spades. Second, a limit raise should show a hand whose *prime feature is good support for partner's suit*. Your excellent club holding dictates the correct action. Bid two clubs (forcing), planning to support spades strongly at your next turn. A limit raise should be employed only when trump support is the salient feature of the hand.

Rebids By Opener

After a limit raise, opening bidder has three possible actions:
a. Pass;
b. Accept partner's game invitation;
c. Try for slam by cue-bidding.

(A pass is jokingly described by some players as showing a hand that ought not to have been opened in the first place. This jest is not far from the truth.) Generally, at rubber bridge or IMPs, you should look for any excuse, however small, to accept the game invitation. The reason is a matter of equities. Assume that game depends on a simple finesse — a fifty-fifty proposition. If you bid a non-vulnerable game and go set, your loss is a 50 point penalty, plus the 140 points you would have gained for a part score — a total of 190 points. If the game contract comes home, you will score 420 points, minus the 170 you would have gained for fulfilling a part score with an overtrick for a profit of 250 points. In other words, you can lose 190 or gain 250.

This relationship is even more dramatic when vulnerable. If you accept the invitation and go set a trick, your loss is 240 points — the 140 you would have picked up for the part score plus the 100 point penalty. If your game contract succeeds, the gain is 450 points — 620 minus the 170 for a part score with an overtrick. Therefore, bidding a 50% vulnerable game risks a potential loss of 240 against a potential gain of 450 — close to two to one odds.

Though any individual hand may go sour, aggressive game bidding, especially when vulnerable, is mathematically correct and, in the long run, winning tactics.

Even at matchpoint duplicate, it is important to bid games with a 50% or better chance to succeed. Assuming that you are playing in a fairly strong game, most of the field will also bid these games — if you do not and the game makes, you will have a very bad board; even if it does not come in, you won't have a bottom.

On occasion you will be dealt a whale of a hand and visions of slam will dance through your head after your partner's limit raise. Give this message to partner by cue bidding an ace in a side suit.

With these options in mind, what do you rebid on each of the following hands after a limit raise by partner?

(1) ♠ K Q 4 3 2   ♡ A J 9 6   ◇ K 6   ♣ 8 5
(One spade — three spades)

Bid four spades. This hand includes only thirteen high card points, but it is nothing to be ashamed of. Your two doubletons are potentially useful and you should be disappointed if game is not close to laydown. Don't bother to work out partner's precise hand. Whatever high cards he holds are likely to be useful for your purposes.

(2) ♠ J 4   ♡ K Q J 7 4   ◇ Q 8 6   ♣ K J 9
(One heart — three hearts)

Pass. Opener should look for any excuse to bid game after a limit raise. In this case, however, there is little excuse to bid on with an aceless thirteen high card point hand. Even the "resident doubleton" found in any five card major suit opening does not constitute a real asset here since it includes one of your high card points. Compare this hand with Example 1; all thirteen high card point hands are not created equal.

(3) ♠ A K 8 6 2   ♡ K 4   ◇ A K J 7   ♣ Q 5
(One spade — three spades)

Four diamonds. With 20 high card points, a strong side suit and distributional advantages, slam is a real possibility. Signal this to partner by cue bidding your outside ace. (A direct leap to Blackwood would be a mistake because you simply don't know enough about responder's hand.)

(4) ♠ 8   ♡ A Q 8 7 4 2   ◇ A J 10 2   ♣ 6 4
(One heart — three hearts)

Four hearts. An absolutely clear-cut bid, despite holding only eleven high card points. This hand is greatly improved by responder's announcement of a heart fit. Even opposite a seemingly useless limit raise:

♠ Q J 3 2   ♡ K 9 6 5   ◇ Q 5   ♣ Q 9 7

game is dependent on a finesse in diamonds. Distribution is a very important consideration when deciding whether or not to carry a limit raise to game.

(5) ♠ Q 9 6 4 2   ♡ 8 4   ◊ A K J 3   ♣ K 3

(One spade — three spades)

Four spades. Don't be deterred by the poor quality of your trump suit. This hand contains the high card values of a full opening bid, plus two potentially useful doubletons. Remember, you don't need much of an excuse to accept the invitation; these two doubletons are enough. Even opposite a minimum limit raise such as:

♠ 8 7 5 3   ♡ A 9 6 3   ◊ 7 6   ♣ A J 5 2

the spade game will succeed if declarer can manage to lose only two trump tricks.

* * *

So far, our choices have been between a sure part score or a possible game. In the next section, we will be choosing between a sure game or a possible slam.

GAME FORCING RAISES

Three Notrump As A Forcing Raise

Every so often responder will hold opening bid values plus good trump support for partner's major suit opening bid. Since the sequences of one heart — three hearts and one spade — three spades are used as invitational raises, we need another way to describe this type of hand. There are several ways to do this — the simplest, hence the most popular, is a direct jump to three notrump.

The requirements for this type of artificial forcing raise are:

(a) At least eleven high card points;

(b) Good trump support, four cards or more;

(c) No long trick producing side suit;

(d) No singletons or voids.

Although (a) and (b) are clear, (c) and (d) require some explanation.

Whenever partner's opening bid virtually assures you of game, you should be alert to the possibility of slam. Assume partner opens with one heart and you hold:

♠ 6 5   ♡ K 8 7 3   ◇ 9 2   ♣ A K Q 5 3

you certainly intend to reach a game in hearts, but your solid five card club suit is sufficient for you to think of something better. If the opening bidder can avoid two immediate losers, slam might be there for the taking — all you have to do is bid it. The correct technique is to bid two clubs, planning to support hearts strongly at your next turn to call.

Similar principles justify the ban against a singleton or a void. Your short suit holding may be the key to producing slam for your partnership. Singleton showing raises will be analyzed presently, but first let's look at a few hands to illustrate the do's and don't's of the three notrump forcing raise.

What is your response to partner's opening bid on each of these hands?

(1) ♠ K Q 6 2   ♡ K 9 8   ◊ Q 4 3   ♣ J 8 7
   (Partner opens with one spade.)

Three spades. Even though eleven high card points is within the range of a forcing raise, this hand more closely meets the qualifications for a limit raise. In this borderline type of situation, examine your hand for extras. These may appear in the shape of useful doubletons, extra trumps or good spot cards. With a 4-3-3-3 flat hand and "soft values," the conservative route is best. If opener cannot find the values to carry on to game, four spades is unlikely to be a good contract.

(2) ♠ A 4   ♡ Q 10 9 7   ◊ A J 10 6   ♣ 9 3 2
   (Partner opens with one heart.)

Three notrump. Another eleven high card point hand, but what a difference! The doubleton spade is likely to produce extra tricks via spade ruffs in dummy and the spot cards in the red suits are good fillers for any possible finesses. Consider yourself unfortunate if four hearts is not a success.

(3) ♠ Q J 8 4 3   ♡ 6 2   ◊ A K J 8   ♣ 8 3
   (Partner opens with one spade.)

Three notrump. As above, eleven high card points should be checked for extra hidden values. In this case, a fifth trump, two doubletons and an excellent source of fast tricks in diamonds are sufficient to demand game. Even to consider a limit raise would be ultra conservative. Hands containing precisely eleven high card points require careful judgment.

(4) ♠ K J 6 5   ♡ A J 8   ◊ K Q 7 5   ♣ Q 3
   (Partner opens with one spade.)

Three notrump. This is a healthy maximum with good trumps. If partner makes any sort of move towards slam, you will be only too happy to cooperate. If partner "signs off" by rebidding four spades, respect his decision. Slam may still be there but it is not likely to be certain. There is nothing more galling than to waste a good hand by spurning a sure game to chase the chimera of a shaky slam.

(5) ♠ **A 8 2**   ♡ **K J 7**   ◊ **K J 3**   ♣ **A J 5 4**

(Partner opens with one heart.)

Two clubs. In old-style bidding, the three notrump response to an opening bid showed the equivalent of a strong notrump opener. Since this bid now is used as a forcing major raise, a temporizing two club response will set the exploratory wheels in motion. Three notrump, indicating a forcing heart raise, would be a mistake here. With 17 high quality points, slam might be cold, even opposite a minimum opening bid. As a general rule, try not to crowd the bidding with very good hands; you need room for exploration.

Optional Treatment

THE JACOBY TWO NOTRUMP RESPONSE
(An Alternative to the Three Notrump Forcing Raise)

Partner deals and bids one heart. Right hand opponent passes and you are looking at one of the following hands:

(a) ♠ A 3   ♡ K 7 5 2   ◇ A J 6 4   ♣ J 8 5
(b) ♠ K J 9   ♡ Q 4   ◇ K Q 10 4   ♣ Q J 9 5

Hand (a) is an easy three notrump response showing a forcing heart raise with no singleton or void. Hand (b) is an old-fashioned two notrump response, looking toward three notrump as the final contract, unless opener indicates a strong preference for suit play.

An interesting alternative to the above is to reverse the meaning of the two bids; i.e., hand (a) bids two notrump to show a forcing heart raise, while hand (b) suggests three notrump by simply bidding three notrump. This concept, developed by the late Oswald Jacoby, has the advantage of supplying an extra level of bidding to explore for slam.

After a sequence of one heart (or one spade) — two notrump, opener's rebid is based on the following schedule of responses:

(a) A new suit at the cheapest level shows a singleton or void in the bid suit.*

(b) A jump to the four level in a new suit shows a strong five card suit.*

(c) A jump to four of the agreed major suit shows a minimum opening bid and denies a strong side suit, a singleton or a void and requests partner to pass unless his original game force contains substantial extra values.

---

*Some players show a singleton with (a) and a void with (b), hoping to be able to show their other long suit, if any, later in the auction. The table given above is somewhat more manageable.

(d) A rebid of three of the agreed major suit denies a singleton or void, but shows enough strength to encourage further investigation by responder.

(e) A raise to three notrump is similar to (d) but shows a "flat" hand with 5-3-3-2 distribution, usually with a weakish trump suit.

Before examining the Jacoby two notrump further, let's try bidding a few hands. Using the preceding schedule of opener's rebids, make the appropriate bid that best describes your hand:

(1) ♠ A Q 6 5 4   ♡ K 8 3   ◇ K J 5   ♣ 7 6

(You have opened one spade, partner has responded two notrump.)

Four spades. While you are quite pleased that partner had the strength to create a game force, you have no interest in slam unless responder has at least an extra ace for his bid. By curtailing investigation with a bid at the four level, you are telling partner that slam is doubtful.

(2) ♠ A J 10 5 4   ♡ 5   ◇ K 9 7 5 4   ♣ A 4

(You have opened one spade; partner has responded two notrump.)

Three hearts. You have a choice to make whether to show your five card diamond suit or your singleton heart. A diamond suit as weak as this is not likely to be a source of tricks unless responder has a diamond fit. For this reason, three hearts, indicating heart shortness, is the best descriptive reply.

(3) ♠ A 4   ♡ A Q 10 7 6   ◇ Q 4   ♣ A K 10 8 5

(You have opened one heart; partner has responded two notrump.)

Four clubs. Again you have a five card side suit, but what difference! Responder needs very little in clubs for this side suit to be worth five tricks. For example, responder may hold:

♠ K 6 5   ♡ K 4 3 2   ◇ A 8 6   ♣ Q 4 3

It's a minimum forcing raise, but sufficient for seven hearts to have excellent chances. This would be a very hard contract for responder to visualize with his 4-3-3-3 shape unless he realizes that his queen of clubs is a valuable asset. The four club bid conveys this message.

(4) ♠ A 5   ♡ K Q 10 8 7 4   ◇ A Q 5   ♣ 7 6

(You have opened one heart; partner has responded two notrump.)

Three hearts. With fifteen high card points, a sixth trump and doubletons in both black suits, your hand certainly contains extra values. By bidding three hearts, you show interest in investigating slam. Remember, with a minimum you would attempt to end the auction by leaping directly to four hearts.

   (5) ♠ A Q J 7 5 4 ♡ — ◇ A J 4 2 ♣ J 8 6
(You have opened one spade; partner has responded two notrump.) Three hearts. This shows heart shortness; if responder exhibits any signs of life, you intend to cue bid hearts again, showing a void (or the singleton ace).

****

Now let's step over to the responder's chair. Opener's response to a Jacoby two notrump bid provides additional information; you can reevaluate your hand based on this information.

If opener indicates a singleton or void, does this gain **effective** ruffing values or is partner's distribution **duplicated** by high cards in your hand? As an example, assume you hold:

   ♠ K 7 6 4 ♡ K Q 9 4 ◇ 6 4 2 ♣ A Q

Partner opens one spade and rebids three hearts over your two notrump forcing raise. Your king-queen of hearts duplicate opener's heart shortness. Because of this unfortunate duplication, slam is unlikely. Reverse the heart-diamond holding:

   ♠ K 7 6 4 ♡ 6 4 2 ◇ K Q 9 4 ♣ A Q

and your hand is much stronger. All of your high cards are "working" and partner's heart shortness is well placed opposite your low cards.

To clarify this point, assume opener's hand is (5) from the last section.

   ♠ A Q J 7 5 4 ♡ — ◇ A J 4 2 ♣ J 8 6
Now examine these two responding hands:

   (a) ♠ K 8 6 4 ♡ K Q 9 3 ◇ 6 5 3 ♣ A Q
A bad slam. Even if the club finesse works, declarer will need a red suit miracle to bring home twelve tricks.

   (b) ♠ K 8 6 4 ♡ 6 5 3 ◇ K Q 9 3 ♣ A Q
A good slam. Six spades is icy; a successful club finesse produces thirteen tricks.*

---

  *Barring a 4-1 diamond split or a spade ruff, a grand slam in diamonds can be made. Don't worry about missing this one; it's almost impossible to bid.

To show lack of slam interest, responder leaps directly to four of the agreed-upon major after opener shows his shortness. As with a jump by opener, this signals lack of interest because it inhibits investigation.

To show slam interest, responder bids something other than four of the opener's major. Common practice is to cue bid the cheapest ace. This signals interest in bigger and better things and asks opener to cue bid in response, beginning a useful exchange of information.

EFFECTIVE POINTS

The concept of effective points must be considered on every hand. If your intermediate honors are opposite partner's short suits, they are of little use. When your ace corresponds with partner's singleton and you have a trump fit, the combined holding cancels out the opponents' high cards, so you can add to your effective point count total to ascertain at what level you wish to play the hand. (Count kings and queens only.)

Evaluate each of the following hands and make your bid in the light of the knowledge gained from opener's communications to you.

(1) ♠ A Q 5 4 ♡ K J 8 7 ◊ A J ♣ J 5 4
     (Partner opened one spade; you bid two notrump;
             partner rebid four spades.)

Pass. Although you hold sixteen high card points, coupled with excellent trump support, respect partner's decision. Opener is showing a minimum hand with no effective distributional values. Slam might be there, but it rates to have a less than even money chance. In the long run, a disciplined pass is the winning call.

(2) ♠ Q J 7 5 4 ♡ 6 4 3 2 ◊ A 8 ♣ A 6
     (Partner opened one spade; you bid two notrump;
             partner rebid three hearts.)

Four clubs. Despite holding only eleven high card points, the forcing raise is quite correct because of a fifth trump and the two doubletons. Opener's announcement of heart shortness has improved your hand dramatically. Assume opener holds:

    ♠ A K 9 8 3 ♡ 5 ◊ K 7 5 ♣ K 5 4 2

A thirteen point minimum, yet a slam should be as easy as pie. Notice that the combined hands contain the prerequisite total number of points for slam.

Combined high card points 24
Effective points — hearts 5
Effective points — diamonds.................... 2
Effective points — clubs....................... 2
                                              ———
TOTAL   33

The nine effective points are based on the fact that the opponents' king-queen of hearts, queen of diamonds and queen of clubs are useless for defensive purposes. The four club cue bid announces your slam intentions.

The decision to express or deny slam interest is a matter of judgment based on several factors:

(a) A trump fit.
(b) High card points.
(c) Effective values.

(3) ♠ K J 5 4   ♡ K 8 6 3   ◇ K J   ♣ Q 6 5
(Partner opened one heart; you responded two notrump;
partner rebid three hearts.)

Four hearts. Having made a forcing raise, you have stated the full value of your hand. If opener has a very good hand, he can bid again. He will know that he is opposite minimum values.

(4) ♠ K 4   ♡ A K 7 6   ◇ K 4 2   ♣ 9 7 4 3
(Partner opened one heart; you bid two notrump;
partner rebid four diamonds.)

Five diamonds. A tough decision. You have no side aces but you hold excellent trumps and your king of diamonds should be a very valuable card. Partner is showing a good five card diamond suit but he does not hold the king, so he is very likely to hold at least the ace-queen. He should not misunderstand your cue bid. If the opponents cannot take two fast tricks in the black suits, a slam is very likely. (Do not fall into the trap of bidding four hearts as a cue bid. Bidding the agreed-upon trump suit at the game level is a signoff with no slam interest.)

(5) ♠ K Q 10   ♡ K Q 6 4   ◇ A 7 5   ♣ 4 3 2
(Partner opened one heart; you bid two notrump;
partner rebid three spades.)

Four hearts. Although you hold a healthy total of fourteen high card points, your hand has deteriorated after partner's response. If your king-queen of spades were elsewhere, it would be "all systems go" for the slam. By bidding four hearts, you tell partner that his singleton spade is duplicated by much of your high card holding. Opener should not bid again without significant extra values.

In general, slam investigation after opener's rebid consists of a series of cue bids in an effort to exchange enough information to determine the advisability of slam.

The following hands illustrate some Jacoby two notrump sequences in action:

North
♠ Q 7 5 4
♡ A 8 7
◊ 4 3
♣ K Q J 4

South
♠ A K 8 6 3 2
♡ K Q 10 4
◊ A 6 2
♣ —

South	North
1 ♠	2 NT
3 ♣[1]	4 ♠[2]
5 ♣[3]	5 ♡[4]
7 ♠[5]	Pass

[1] Showing a singleton or void in clubs.
[2] With half his strength in clubs, North devalues his hand and signs off in game.
[3] South is too strong to accept a sign off. By bidding five clubs, South shows first round club control.
[4] Cue bidding the ace of hearts.
[5] An aggressive though well considered try for a big score.

As the cards lie, the grand slam has a first rate play despite the club duplication. After drawing trumps, declarer can test the hearts. If the jack drops, he can pitch a diamond from dummy. If not, he can try a ruffing finesse in clubs.

North
- ♠ A K 5 4
- ♡ 6 5
- ◊ A Q 7 6
- ♣ Q 3 2

South
- ♠ Q J 8 3 2
- ♡ A K 7
- ◊ K 9 4 3
- ♣ 5

South	North
1 ♠	2 NT
3 ♣[1]	3 ◊[2]
3 ♡[3]	3 ♠[4]
4 ◊[5]	4 NT[6]
5 ♡[7]	6 ♠[8]
Pass	

[1]Showing a singleton or void in clubs.

[2]Cue bidding the ace of diamonds. Although the queen of clubs is a duplicated value, North has full opening values outside partner's singleton — a good indication of slam possibilities.

[3]Cue bidding the ace of hearts.

[4]A temporizing but forward going call. To show lack of interest, North would jump directly to four spades. By bidding only three spades, North leaves South maximum room to further describe his hand.

[5]Cue bidding the king of diamonds. Please notice that both partners know that there is a sure club loser. (With the ace or a void, South would cue bid four clubs.)

[6]A delicate bid. Most emphatically not Blackwood. Since the partnership is involved in a cue bidding sequence, Blackwood would be a redundancy. This is a request for further information; from North's point of view, slam depends on partner's heart holding.

[7]South cue bids his heart king, completing the description of his hand. North now knows that South holds the ace-king of hearts and the king of diamonds.

[8]Armed with all this information, North can visualize a slam that should have excellent chances of success. Although his queen of clubs is a duplicated value, the distribution neutralizes the king of clubs and the queen of hearts, adding effective points to the combined partnership assets, putting them well within slam range.

Evaluation

The Jacoby two notrump convention enables a partnership to evaluate slam potential at a low level. The only drawback is its complexity; although it provides greater accuracy than the three notrump forcing raise, it takes time to learn the responses and understand their nuances. If you don't mind paying this price, the Jacoby two notrump is a definite plus in your quest for accurate bidding.

SPLINTER BIDS

A splinter bid is a different type of forcing raise, used to locate shortness. It is a double jump in a suit (other than partner's major), showing a forcing raise in the major, coupled with a singleton or void in the bid suit.

One heart — three spades	= Forcing heart raise with spade shortness
One heart — four clubs	= Forcing heart raise with club shortness
One heart — four diamonds	= Forcing heart raise with diamond shortness
One spade — four clubs	= Forcing spade raise with club shortness
One spade — four diamonds	= Forcing spade raise with diamond shortness
One spade — four hearts	= Forcing spade raise with heart shortness

The requirements for a splinter bid are:
(a) A singleton or void in the bid suit;
(b) Support (four cards or more) for partner's major suit;
(c) Game-going values;
(d) No long trick-producing side suit.

With very few exceptions, it is bad practice to splinter with only three trumps. Since astute defenders normally lead trumps against a splinter auction to cut down dummy's ruffing power, a fourth trump makes all the difference in the world.

As with the three notrump raise, the decision on borderline hands between a splinter and a limit raise is based on the quality of the points. Control cards and good general texture are positive factors. Unsupported queens and jacks are negative factors.

A side suit singleton or void may be a virtually meaningless asset if it is opposite partner's high cards, or it may be a critical positive factor for slam if partner's side suit values are elsewhere. The following hand illustrates this principle:

North
♠ K 8 6 3
♡ 8
◇ A J 7 3
♣ A 8 6 3

South
♠ A Q J 5 2
♡ K Q 10 4
◇ 6 5 4
♣ 2

With spades as trump, South must lose one heart and one or two diamonds, depending on the lie of the cards. But switch dummy's red suit holdings and notice the dramatic difference.

North
♠ K 8 6 3
♡ A J 7 3
◇ 8
♣ A 8 6 3

In the first case, South's heart honors are duplicated by North's singleton; both holdings prevent two heart losers. In the second case, the defense holds A-K-Q of diamonds but only the ace is useful on defense.

(A) If a singleton or void is opposite a high card concentration, it is a duplicated value.

(B) If a singleton or void is opposite partner's low cards, with the high cards in a more useful place, it is an effective value.

Now try these five situations. What is your response to partner's opening bid?

(1) ♠ A Q 9 6 ♡ K 8 4 3 ◇ Q J 3 2 ♣ 7
(Partner opens one heart.)

Four clubs. This is the classic splinter bid. With one call you've told partner that you have a forcing raise and a singleton or void in clubs, providing extra tricks via club ruffs in dummy.

(2) ♠ K J 8 6 ♡ 5 ◇ Q 10 8 4 2 ♣ A 7 3
(Partner opens one spade.)

Four hearts. With ten high card points, you must decide between a conservative limit raise and an aggressive game forcing bid. Since you have excellent trump support, an outside ace and a potentially useful five card suit, a game forcing splinter is the correct action. Partner may hold a totally inappropriate hand:

♠ A Q 10 3 2 ♡ K J 6 3 ◇ 7 3 ♣ Q 2

in which case, game is a bad bet. In the long run, however, an aggressive posture in these situations should prove to be the winning action.

(3) ♠ K Q J 6 ♡ Q 8 5 2 ◇ Q 7 6 4 ♣ 6
(Partner opens one spade.)

Three spades. This is a good limit raise, but an overaggressive splinter bid. ALTHOUGH YOU HOLD EXCELLENT TRUMP SUPPORT, YOU HAVE LITTLE TO OFFER IN THE WAY OF SIDE SUIT STRENGTH. Remember, opener will look for any excuse to bid game over a limit raise. If he cannot find one, then four spades is not likely to be a good contract.

(4) ♠ 7 ♡ Q 10 8 7 ◇ Q 3 ♣ A K J 8 3 2
(Partner opens one heart.)

Two clubs. You hold the values for a game force in hearts, but your hand may be too good! You have two potential assets, either of which may be sufficient to produce slam: the singleton spade and a practically solid club suit. The splinter bid puts too many of your eggs in one basket, because it takes up too much bidding room. Opener may hold something like:

♠ K 6 5 ♡ A K 6 4 2 ◇ A 5 4 ♣ 6 5

Six hearts is an odds-on contract, but opener will doubtless sign off in four. (More about this type of hand later. For the moment, realize that with two excellent sources of tricks, you would be misleading partner by stating that your main asset, in addition to the values for a forcing raise, is a singleton spade.)

(5) ♠ K J 8 7   ♡ K J 6 3   ◊ —   ♣ K 9 6 4 3
(Partner opens one heart.)

Four diamonds. Splintering with a void can be a dangerous business since the difference between a singleton and a void is of critical importance when considering the possibility of slam. As an example, assume opener holds the ace of diamonds. If you hold a singleton, it is a useful card. If you have a void, it is a useless duplication. As a general rule, a splinter bid with a void should include minimum high card values. With a better hand, you should temporize by bidding another suit.

Now let's change seats. You open the bidding either one heart or one spade. Partner responds with a splinter bid and you have a decision to make. Should you sign off by rebidding your major or attempt to reach a slam? This is a matter of judgment, aided by a knowledge of the principle of duplicated values versus effective values. Consider the following combined holdings:

North
♠ K 10 9 8
♡ 8
◊ A Q 8 7
♣ A 10 7 2

South
♠ A Q J 5 4
♡ K J 3
◊ 5 4 2
♣ K 5

With spades as trump, South's heart king will prevent the opponents from garnering two immediate heart tricks; the singleton heart in the North hand performs the same function. When high cards perform the same function as distribution in a given hand, these high cards are **duplicated values.**

Interchanging South's red suit holdings makes a dramatic difference.

North
- ♠ K 10 9 8
- ♡ 8
- ◊ A Q 8 7
- ♣ A 10 7 2

South
- ♠ A Q J 5 4
- ♡ 5 4 2
- ◊ K J 3
- ♣ K 5

Now North's singleton heart is an **effective value** since South holds three heart losers.

In the first case, four spades is makeable with minimum care; in the second case twelve tricks are there for the taking.

Note that North-South hold a combined 27 high card points, but the rule of 33 points for a small slam is not violated. Due to the effective points of the second pair of hands, the king-queen of hearts and the queen of clubs will be ruffed away. Adding these seven points to the total brings this hand well within slam range.

With this in mind, exercise your judgment on the following hands, remembering that an effective holding is an asset while duplicated holdings are a liability.

(1) ♠ K Q 10   ♡ A Q 10 6 2   ◊ Q 10   ♣ J 5 3

North	East	South	West
1 ♡	Pass	3 ♠	Pass
?			

Four hearts. Partner's singleton spade has added no effective points to your total holdings because your king-queen of spades are a duplication. Three small spades would be better; if your outside high cards were in the minors, you would have a first-rate slam try. Simply sign off in game and tell partner that his splinter bid did not improve your hand. (In a duplicate tournament, three notrump is a possible call.)

(2) ♠ K Q 10 7 3   ♡ K 6   ◇ A Q 5   ♣ 9 4 3

North	East	South	West
1♠	Pass	4♣	Pass
?			

Four diamonds. Although this hand contains only fourteen high card points, it is well worth a slam try. Assume partner holds an average forcing raise, about twelve high card points. With partner's singleton club, the opponents will score the ace, but their king-queen will be ruffed away by dummy's trumps. This adds five points to your total effective points*, putting you well within slam range.

(3) ♠ A K 5 3 2   ♡ Q J 10 6   ◇ Q 7   ♣ A Q

North	East	South	West
1♠	Pass	4 ♡	Pass
?			

Five clubs. Despite the duplication in hearts, this hand is still worth a slam try. To determine whether or not a hand containing duplicated values is worth a move toward slam, count only the ace of the splinter suit (if you hold it), plus your other high card points. If these values still total an opening bid, the hand is worth investigating further. Compare this to hand (1) which contains only nine high card points outside the splinter suit (spades), and is not worth a slam try after a spade splinter by partner.

(4) ♠ A K 8 6 2   ♡ A Q 9 3   ◇ 9 6 5 3   ♣ —

North	East	South	West
1♠	2♡	4◇	Pass
?			

Four hearts. Partner's four diamond response is still a splinter despite East's two heart overcall. Here is an easy rule to identify a splinter bid: If a simple bid (in this case, three diamonds) would have been forcing, then a jump shows a singleton or void.

---

*To play safe with effective point counting, count aces, kings and queens, but not jacks. This will give you a solid safety margin. Also, if the defense has a cashable trick in a suit, assume they will take this trick with their highest card. Thus, if declarer has three low cards opposite a singleton in dummy, the defenders can win the ace of this suit, but not the king-queen.

Tread gently with this auction; you may have two sure losers — the ace of diamonds plus a heart. (Assume a diamond singleton rather than a void.)

(5) ♠ Q 6 5 3 2   ♡ A 7 3   ◇ 3   ♣ A K 4 2

North	East	South	West
1♠	Pass	4♡	Pass
?			

Five clubs. As before, evaluate the strength of your hand in relation to the splinter bid. Since you have no duplication in hearts (assuming a singleton rather than a void), a cue bid is appropriate. Don't worry about the poor quality of your trumps; partner should have the necessary fillers as part of his game forcing raise.

A bit of advice regarding splinter bids: should you add splinters to your bidding system, there is a real chance that your favorite partner (not you, of course) will forget. The auction will be something like:

North	East	South	West
1♠	Pass	4♡	Pass
Pass	Pass	Pass	

Don't worry, it will only happen once! The humiliation of languishing in a 3-1 trump fit will insure against such an accident occurring again.

Splinter bids can also be employed in other sequences. A double jump by the opener would show four card support for responder's suit plus a singleton or void in the suit bid.

Opener	Responder
1♣	1♡
3◇	

or

1♣	1♠
3◇	

Since a diamond bid at one level lower would be forcing in either of the above sequences, the double jump has no meaning in standard bidding. (Naturally, the opener must have enough strength to want to play game in responder's suit.)

There is also a delayed splinter bid, whereby responder can show four card support for opener's second suit plus a singleton or void in the bid suit:

Opener	Responder
1♠	2♣
2♡	4♢

should show four card heart support plus a singleton diamond, since a three diamond bid would be forcing.

* * *

So far, we have examined direct raises in ascending order to strength. Now we do an abrupt about-face and look at hands with excellent distribution coupled with under-average high card strength.

THE PREEMPTIVE JUMP TO GAME

Partner opens the bidding with one heart and you hold the following array:

♠ 6   ♡ J 8 4 3 2   ◊ A 8 7 6 4 2   ♣ 9

Two things are obvious. First, your combined assets provide excellent offensive possibilities with hearts as trump. Second, you can offer little in the way of defense should the opponents declare this hand in either black suit. In fact, your defensive values are negative because of heart length; the opponents will be able to ruff away your partner's high hearts. Opener may hold something like:

♠ J 8 3   ♡ A K Q 10 7   ◊ K Q 5 3   ♣ 2

A healthy opening bid, yet the opponents will take between eleven and thirteen tricks in the black suits. This example is a bit extreme — all of your defensive values are duplicated, but the principle is obvious: You would much rather declare than defend.

A direct jump to four of partner's major suit combines the best features of preemption and aggression. Your hand may be just shapely enough to produce ten tricks and the opponents must brave the dangers of entering the auction at the four level. And, should partner hold a better defensive hand, something like:

♠ K Q 10   ♡ A 9 7 6 5   ◊ 5   ♣ K Q 10 2

he will be able to punish any attempt by the opponents to get involved.

The following are some guidelines for the preemptive jump to game:

(a) At least four card trump support;
(b) A singleton or void;
(c) Outside high cards, if any, in a long side suit;
(d) Few, if any, "soft" values;
(e) Less than nine high card points.

The necessity for at least four trumps is coupled with the requirement of a singleton or void. Opener must be able to take tricks by ruffing in dummy, so provide him with enough trumps to do so.

Similarly, values in a long side suit are more desirable than possible defensive tricks in short suits. To illustrate, if partner has opened the bidding with one spade, this hand:

♠ Q 10 8 4   ♡ 3   ◇ 6 5 4   ♣ K J 8 6 3

is a much better preemptive hand than:

♠ Q 10 8 4   ♡ 3   ◇ K 5 4   ♣ J 8 6 3 2

The ideal preemptive jump combines all five of the above mentioned principles. Unfortunately, the Lord in His wisdom seldom deals us the perfect hand and we have to compromise with perfection.

What would you bid with each of the following not completely ideal hands? In each case you are seated South:

(1) ♠ K 8 6 3 2   ♡ 9 7 4 2   ◇ 8 6 5 2   ♣ —

North	East	South	West
1♠	Pass	?	

Four spades. Although this hand does not contain any sort of long suit, your utter lack of defense should impel you to leap to four spades in desperation. Perhaps you may be pleasantly surprised, but don't be disappointed if partner goes down. The important thing is that you have blocked the enemy lines of communication. On balance, East-West probably hold more aces and kings than you and partner, but if they want to compete they must begin their exploration at the five level. This could be dangerous since partner may hold a hand suitable to double anything they bid.

A very important point — if partner does double, do not consider removing to five spades. You have pointed out the defenseless nature of your hand in one bid. Now you must trust partner.

(2) ♠ 6   ♡ K 9 5 4 2   ◇ A K J 8 7   ♣ 6 5

North	East	South	West
1♡	Pass	?	

Two diamonds. With a hand as strong as this, your thoughts should be closer to slam than preemption. Partner might be looking at:

♠ A 5 4   ♡ A 8 7 6 3   ◇ Q 3 2   ♣ A 4

He will certainly pass four hearts; barring a three-zero trump split or a five-zero diamond break, he will just as certainly score all of the tricks.

(3) ♠ K J 5   ♡ 5   ◇ 8 6 4 2   ♣ K 7 5 4 3

North	East	South	West
1♠	Pass	?	

Two spades. It is very dangerous to preempt with only three trumps. You don't have enough ruffing values to make many tricks, and there is no evidence that your high spades will not produce defensive tricks. Your hand is not as bad as it looks. If partner makes a help-suit game try of three clubs or three hearts, you should leap directly to game in spades, since you have excellent help in both suits. Of course, if partner tries with three diamonds, you should discreetly retreat to three spades; your four diamonds are not what he needs.

(4) ♠ 7   ♡ K J 8 7   ◇ 9 8 7   ♣ A Q 5 3 2

North	East	South	West
1♡	2♣	?	

Four hearts. It is very likely that you can punish two clubs, but it is even more probably that East-West will retreat to spades, since it is certain that they have at least an eight card spade fit; your job is to keep then from finding it.* This hand is on the strongish side, but a splinter bid would be inappropriate since the auction hints that the suits aren't going to break. Also, from a preemptive point of view, you may do tactical damage to your chances of buying the contract by highlighting your shortness in spades, e.g.:

North	East	South	West
1♡	2♣	3♠	Dbl!

West's double suggests a spade contract to East at no risk.

(5) ♠ 6   ♡ K J 6 4   ◇ 7 3 2   ♣ 9 6 4 3 2

North	East	South	West
1♡	2♣	?	

So far we have not considered vulnerability. With any level of pre-emptive bid, vulnerability is a key factor. If you are not vulnerable, four hearts is a clear-cut call on this hand. East-West cannot know whether you are bidding four hearts from weakness or from

---

*The danger of an East-West spade fit is more pronounced if your partnership uses the Flannery convention, to be discussed later.

strength. If vulnerable, however, four hearts would be questionable except against the most timid opponents. You are almost certain to be doubled and may go down more than the value of East-West's probable game. Try two hearts and see how the auction proceeds.

Summary

A direct raise of partner's opening major suit bid is normally the simplest and smoothest road to the proper contract.

Weakish hands with three or more trumps and no outstanding distributional features are best described by a raise to the two level. This bid is non-constructive; opener needs better than minimum values to press on. The same high card count with four or more trumps plus useful distribution, such as singletons or voids, is usually best described by a direct jump to game. (This bid should never be used with a strong hand, because it may well preempt partner rather than the opponents.)

A single jump in partner's major suit is a limit raise, non-forcing though highly encouraging. The limit raise promises four trumps and approximately ten or eleven points in support of opener's major suit. Opener should strain to carry on to game.

The forcing raise can be made in two ways:

(1) Three notrump (or optionally Jacoby two notrump) promises four trumps, a hand with no singleton or void and opening bid values. Opener can either sign off in game or probe for slam via cue bids, Blackwood or other slam conventions. (More on slam exploration later.)

(2) With four trumps and a singleton or void in a side suit, responder can utilize a splinter bid. Opener should analyze his hand in the light of responder's bid and determine whether his hand contains effective points or duplicated values. With effective points, he should try for slam; with duplicated points, he signs off in four of his own suit.

TWO VITAL CONVENTIONS

An argument often presented by four card majorites is that unless a number of conventions are employed a five card major structure is unwieldy due to the occasional necessity to start the bidding with a three card minor. There is a grain of truth to this objection, for it is necessary to employ at least two conventions to use a five card major structure accurately — the forcing notrump and the negative double. Any partnership that plays five card majors without these conventions is playing an incomplete system and will be confronted by many problems.

THE FORCING NOTRUMP

Standard bidding boasts an almost completely natural structure. One of the few artificial bids, however, is the response of one notrump to a major suit opening bid, which can show many different hands, not necessarily notrump-oriented. If partner opens one spade you would respond one notrump with any of the following hands:

1. ♠ 5 4 ♡ K 10 8 4 ◇ A J 5 4 3 ♣ 7 6

2. ♠ Q 5 ♡ 3 ◇ J 5 4 3 ♣ A J 9 7 6 5

3. ♠ — ♡ A 9 6 4 3 2 ◇ J 5 4 3 ♣ Q 6 4

4. ♠ Q 2 ♡ J 3 2 ◇ 5 ♣ Q J 10 9 6 4 2

5. ♠ J ♡ K J 8 4 ◇ K 10 5 3 ♣ Q 10 4 2

Assume that the opener holds:

♠ A K 8 6 3   ♡ Q 7 5   ◇ Q 8 6   ♣ K 3

With this flat 14 high card points, he would pass. Analyzing each hand, we find that on hand (1), one notrump is in jeopardy, especially after a club lead. A diamond partial would be a much safer contract. Hand (2) is also suit-oriented; two clubs or even two spades would be better contracts. Hand (3) would be best in two hearts but there is no logical way to get there. Hand (4) poses similar problems — the diamond suit is wide open and one notrump is unlikely to be a success story. Clubs would be a nice place to play this hand but responder is much too weak for a two club response. Only on hand (5) is one notrump a good contract.

To solve this problem, modern five card majorities use the one notrump response as a forcing bid after a major suit opening by partner. Opener must bid again, allowing responder to define his hand further.

FORCING NOTRUMP RULES

(1) A one notrump response is forcing after partner's major suit opening bid.

North	East	South	West
1♠	Pass	1 NT	

is forcing; opener must bid again.

North	East	South	West
1 ◇	Pass	1 NT	

is not forcing; North opened with a minor suit.

(2) The forcing notrump response normally shows five to eleven high card points.

(3) The forcing notrump only applies in noncompetitive auctions.

North	East	South	West
1 ♡	Pass	1 NT	

is forcing.

North	East	South	West
1 ♡	1♠	1 NT	

is natural and nonforcing, showing seven to ten high card points, spade stoppers, and notrump distribution.

Opener's rebid can be of four different types:

(a) The original major. This promises at least six cards in the suit; there is seldom any reason to rebid a five card suit. The level of the rebid is dependent on the strength of the hand. Assume that you have opened with one spade and partner responds with one notrump. Looking at:

    ♠ A K J 8 4 3 ♡ K 7 2 ◇ Q 6 4 ♣ 3

a two spade rebid best describes this minimum range hand. Change it to something such as:

    ♠ A K Q 6 4 3 ♡ K 7 2 ◇ A 7 3 ♣ 9

And three spades would be correct, showing a better than minimum opening with six good spades — invitational and nonforcing. Add one more spade, giving:

♠ A K Q 8 6 4 2   ♡ K 2   ◇ A 7 3   ♣ 9

The correct rebid with this 8½ trick hand is four spades.

(b) The other major. This promises at least four cards in that suit. The sequence;

North	East	South	West
1 ♠	Pass	1 NT	Pass
2 ♡			

shows five spades and at least four hearts and is nonforcing.

However, the auction:

North	East	South	West
1 ♡	Pass	1 NT	Pass
2 ♠			

is forcing for one round, since there is no reason to show a four card spade suit with minimum values, because the notrump response denies a four card spade suit. The only reason for a two spade rebid is to indicate extra values.

The one hand which is hard to handle using the forcing notrump is the holding of four spades, five hearts and doubletons in both minors, with a minimum opening bid. A special bid called Flannery (discussed later in this book) is used by many players to announce this holding. If you do not wish to add another convention to your system at this time, then just rebid the five card heart suit — it is better to misrepresent the length of the major suit than to lie about the strength of the hand.

(c) A minor suit. This ordinarily shows four or more cards in the suit, but with a hand such as:

♠ A K 6 5 3   ♡ A 7 4   ◇ 9 2   ♣ K 8 3

two clubs is the only available rebid. Don't be afraid to rebid a three card minor; partner is aware of this possibility.

(d) Raise notrump. This shows extra values and no second suit four cards or longer. A raise to two notrump is game invitational, showing approximately 16 to 18 high card points, e.g.,

♠ A K J 4 2   ♡ K Q 4   ◇ K J 8   ♣ 7 6

An original notrump opening with this hand is not appetizing because of the glaring weakness in clubs, but opener should raise to two notrump in response to partner's one notrump. Give opener a slightly stronger hand:

♠ A K J 4 2 ♡ K Q 4 ◇ K 8 6 ♣ K 7

and he would proceed directly to three notrump. This shows a hand too good to open with one notrump and too weak for two notrump.

Using the above descriptions as guidelines, consider your rebid on each of the following five hands. In each case, you have opened the bidding in the indicated major and partner has responded with a forcing notrump.

(1) ♠ A Q 6 5 3 ♡ K Q 7 4 2 ◇ Q 9 ♣ 8
  (One spade — one notrump.)

Two hearts. An easy rebid, whether or not you play forcing notrump. Partner will know you hold five spades and at least four hearts; if you get another chance to bid, you will show the five card heart suit by rebidding it.

(2) ♠ A K 8 2 ♡ A K J 4 2 ◇ 7 ♣ K 9 6
  (One heart — one notrump.)

Two spades. The correct bid with this excellent hand to show your partner extra values and force him to bid again. His rebid will provide you with a better indication of the potential of the hand.

(3) ♠ A 6 ♡ J 10 4 3 2 ◇ A 8 2 ♣ A K J
  (One heart — one notrump.)

Two notrump. (Most experts would have opened one notrump with such a weak five card major.) By rebidding two notrump, you give partner the option to pass, to bid three notrump or introduce his long suit. (The last alternative will be discussed in the next section.)

(4) ♠ K Q J 6 ♡ A K 7 4 3 ◇ J 9 2 ♣ 9
  (One heart — one notrump.)

Two diamonds. A rebid of two spades would exaggerate the strength of this minimum range opening. Rebidding a three card suit headed by the jack may seem a bit heady at first, but partner is aware of this possibility.

(5) ♠ K Q J 10 6 2 ♡ 7 ◇ A 7 ♣ A Q 10 6
  (One spade — one notrump.)

Three spades. Again, bidding is a pragmatic business and we would bypass the four card suit in favor of the more descriptive jump rebid in spades. If there is a game, spades is the most likely candidate.

REBIDS BY RESPONDER

You may ask, "So what? What have we gained by using a one notrump forcing response?" Primarily, since opener is forced to rebid, responder can now describe his hand with great accuracy. Among his rebid options are:

(1) Bid a new suit. This shows length in that suit, but denies the strength for an original two over one bid. For example, holding:

♠ — ♡ A 8 6 5 4 3 ◇ J 7 3 2 ♣ Q 6 4

The auction might proceed as follows:

North	South
1 ♠	1 NT
2 ◇	2 ♡

which describes a weak hand with length in hearts. (You would not pass two diamonds since declarer might have only a three card suit.) Or:

♠ Q 6 ♡ J 5 4 ◇ 9 ♣ Q J 10 9 6 4 2

North	South
1 ♠	1 NT
2 ◇	3 ♣

which again shows a weak hand with a long suit.

(2) Rebid two notrump, showing ten or eleven high card points and invitational to three notrump. This is a very useful bid; it is no longer necessary to manufacture a two over one call to show strength. Suppose you hold:

♠ J 6 ♡ K J 5 ◇ K 10 9 3 ♣ Q 10 6 4

and partner opens with one spade. Playing a nonforcing notrump, a one notrump response is slightly conservative while a two club or two diamond bid would be aggressive. Playing forcing notrump, you can tell the whole story by bidding one notrump followed by two notrump.

(3) With no long suit of your own and inadequate strength to rebid two notrump, it is normally correct to return to the original major with a doubleton. With:

♠ Q 6   ♡ K 7 5 4   ◇ K 3 2   ♣ 10 6 4 3

The auction might be:

North	South
1 ♠	1 NT
2 ◇	2 ♠

(It would be dangerous to pass two diamonds since partner may hold only three cards in the suit. Two spades will probably play as well as one notrump, especially if partner started with a short club holding).

(4) The jump raise of partner's first bid suit shows a limit raise (ten to twelve points) with only three trumps.

♠ J 6 4   ♡ A 7 3   ◇ A Q 9 2   ♣ 6 5 2

North	South
1 ♠	1 NT
2 ♣	3 ♠

(A direct limit raise, one spade — three spades or one heart — three hearts, guarantees a four card trump holding.)

(5) By employing the forcing notrump, responder often finds out helpful information about partner's hand. Assume you hold:

♠ 8   ♡ 10 7 3 2   ◇ 10 6 4 2   ♣ K Q 5 2

Partner opens with one spade and rebids two diamonds in response to your forcing notrump. You would pass, confident that you have reached a good contract. With a somewhat better hand:

♠ 8   ♡ Q 10 7 3   ◇ K 10 6 4 2   ♣ A 5 2

and after the same sequence of bidding (one spade — one notrump — two diamonds), a raise to three diamonds indicates a maximum notrump response with excellent trump support, even allowing for a three card suit in partner's hand. This gives a very accurate description of your hand and allows partner to make the next move.

Now try a few rebid problems:

(1) ♠ A 8   ♡ K J 6 3   ◊ J 10 8 2   ♣ 7 5 2

North	South
1 ♠	1 NT
2 ♡	?

Three hearts. This is invitational to game, showing nine to eleven points and four card heart support. Your hand has been improved by the bidding and the possibility of game should not be overlooked.

(2) ♠ 9   ♡ K J 8 6 4 3 2   ◊ 8 4   ♣ Q 7 2

North	South
1 ♠	1 NT
2 NT	?

Four hearts. Opposite a one notrump opening bid, you would have no hesitation in leaping to a heart game. Opener has a notrump opening with a five card spade suit. Although four hearts may not make, a signoff bid of three hearts would be ultra conservative.

(3) ♠ 6 5   ♡ J 8   ◊ A Q 9 2   ♣ K 9 4 3 2

North	South
1 ♠	1 NT
2 ♣	?

Three clubs. This invitational bid guarantees a five card suit because opener may well hold only three clubs. Barring a very distributional opening bid, the invitation is primarily aimed at the possibility of three notrump. A rebid of two notrump would be a mistake because of the weakness in hearts.

(4) ♠ 8 4 3   ♡ K 7   ◊ 7 6 5 3   ♣ A 10 8 2

North	South
1 ♡	1 NT
2 ♠	?

Three hearts. Opener has shown a very strong hand by reversing and it is your duty to bid again. Despite the fact that you hold only seven high card points, your hand is quite good. The ace of clubs is surely useful and the king of hearts has to be a welcome asset. Since you failed to raise hearts directly, partner should be aware of the possibility that you have only a doubleton heart.

(5) ♠ Q J 3   ♡ K J 6 3   ◊ K 10 8 3   ♣ 7 4

North	South
1 ♠	1 NT
2 ◊	?

Three spades. This shows a limit raise with only three trumps.

CONSTRUCTIVE RAISES

Understanding the forcing notrump opens the door to some interesting tactical bidding sequences. As an example, assume you are dealt the following depressing array:

♠ J 5 3   ♡ J 4 3 2   ◇ K J 5 3   ♣ 10 7

Partner opens with one spade and you have just enough to scrape together a raise to two spades. However, there is a trap to this hand. If partner has a good enough hand to fulfill his contract in comfort, he probably will either try for game or leap directly to game, getting your side too high for a plus score.

One way around this is to utilize the forcing notrump response. Bid one notrump, planning to return to spades at your next chance, showing a weak hand. Now the minimum requirement for a single raise becomes eight points, known as a **constructive raise.**

The rules for the constructive raise are very simple:

(1) The simple raise — one heart/spade — two hearts/spades shows eight to a poor ten points in support of opener's major.

(2) With five to seven points in support of partner's suit, responder first bids one notrump and then bids the minimum number of partner's major at his next turn to call.

(3) The constructive raise is only applicable in non-competitive auctions. Thus:

North	East	South	West
1 ♠	Pass	2 ♠	

is constructive, while:

North	East	South	West
1 ♠	2 ◇	2 ♠	

is merely competitive.

The constructive raise is an excellent descriptive bid, increasing the accuracy of your bidding while giving away very little.

The following five hands are designed to test your understanding of the constructive raise. In each case, partner has opened the bidding with one heart. What is the correct response?

(1) ♠ J 5   ♡ K Q 7 2   ♢ 10 5 4   ♣ 7 4 3 2

One notrump. You are a trifle weak for a direct raise to two hearts. If the opponents compete, you intend to fight for the contract, but not very hard. If partner does not show signs of life, the opponents may well have game — possibly in spades.

(2) ♠ K 7   ♡ K J 10 5   ♢ 3 2   ♣ 9 7 5 3 2

Two hearts. Although you hold only seven high card points this hand qualifies as a constructive raise. Remember, these are points in support of hearts; your two doubletons are sufficient to bring your hand well into the constructive raise range.

(3) ♠ 3   ♡ 9 7 5 4 3   ♢ A 5 4 3 2   ♣ 7 4

Four hearts. The fact that you've adopted constructive raises does not affect any normal call except the simple raise. This is a clear cut preemptive hand and four hearts is your best call.

(4) ♠ Q 8 7   ♡ J 5 4 2   ♢ A Q 7   ♣ J 7 3

Two hearts. Although you hold ten high card points the shape of this hand will be a disappointment for partner. A single constructive raise is sufficient.

(5) ♠ J 5 4 3   ♡ A 8 4   ♢ 3 2   ♣ A 10 7 6

Two hearts. With two aces and a potential ruffing value in diamonds, this is a forward-going hand best described by the constructive raise. If the spade-heart holding were reversed, we would opt for a limit raise; with only three trumps, the constructive raise is the best bet.

Now give your imagination free rein on this next set of hands. Then make the master call to land your partnership in the master contract.

(1) ♠ A J   ♡ 8 6 4   ♢ 9 2   ♣ K J 7 6 5 3

North	South
1 ♠	1 NT
2 ♣	?

Four spades. This contract could range from ice cold to unmakable. Your side has a double fit in the black suits which offers a very exciting potential. The results could be quite startling. Opener might have started with:

♠ K Q 9 7 3   ♡ 5   ◊ Q 7 6   ♣ A Q 8 2

Your side is odds on to fulfill a spade game, while five clubs is unmakable and the opponents may well be able to make four hearts. Of course, opener may hold:

♠ K 7 6 5 4   ♡ Q 7 3   ◊ K J   ♣ A 4 2

and four spades is tenuous at best. Nevertheless, we prefer this "swingy" jump to game to a more solid though less forward-going raise to three clubs.

(2) ♠ 6   ♡ K 5   ◊ A J 8 7 4 3   ♣ Q 10 6 2

North	South
1 ♠	1 NT
2 ◊	?

Three notrump. Despite holding ten high card points and a long suit, a forcing one notrump response is the only correct action. The lack of a fit with opener warns of caution because the hand may turn out to be a massive misfit. Over two clubs or two hearts, responder had planned to rebid two notrump but, after the pleasantly surprising two diamond rebid by opener, responder has a good chance for six diamond tricks. Three notrump is most definitely a "maybe" contract. Assume opener holds:

♠ A K 8 5 2   ♡ J 7   ◊ K Q 2   ♣ J 5 4

A club lead followed by a heart shift might well skewer the contract. However, this is a hard defense to find in view of the uninformative auction. Against a more likely heart lead, nine tricks can be gathered easily. A simple raise to three diamonds would not do justice to the trick-taking potential of this hand. Note that South should play the hand in notrump, since he has a sure stopper with an opening heart lead.

(3) ♠ 7   ♡ 8 4   ◊ A J 8 6 5 4   ♣ K J 7 2

North	South
1 ♡	1 NT
2 ◊	?

Two spades. If you held a spade suit, you would have responded one spade to partner's bid. Therefore, opener should interpret this unusual call as signalling an excellent fit for diamonds with a spade control. If opener subsequently rebids three hearts, he would be showing an excellent five card suit and you should try four hearts. If he rebids two notrump, return to three diamonds and leave the next move to him. *Always be aware when the auction improves your hand and strive to make the strongest possible rebid.* (Don't try this bid with an inexperienced pickup partner — it is only included here to show what imaginative auctioneering the forcing notrump lends itself to.)

(4) ♠ 9 3　♡ —　◇ Q 9 6 4　♣ J 10 6 5 4 3 2

North	South
1 ♡	?

One notrump. If you were not playing the forcing notrump, you would probably pass one heart. Utilizing the forcing notrump, your plan is to try for a club part score. This is a real hand from a Swiss Team event. Opener held:

♠ A 8 2　♡ A K 9 6 5　◇ 7　♣ A K 7 6

At one table, the contract was one heart, making six tricks. At the other table the auction went:

North	South
1 ♡	1 NT!
3 ♣	5 ♣!
6 ♣	

and the small slam came rolling home with the loss of one diamond trick. This is an extreme situation, but delightful things like this can happen.

(5) ♠ 8 3 2　♡ Q 7 6 3　◇ Q 4 3　♣ Q 9 2

North	South
1 ♡	?

One notrump. The first four hands were examples of using the forcing notrump without a fit in partner's suit. This hand is an attempt to dilute his possibly aggressive intentions. With three queens, no distributional plusses and no spot cards, you are as minimum as you could possibly be. A direct raise to two hearts is likely to elicit some sort of game try by partner. After your initial one notrump response, you plan to return to hearts at every opportunity, declining any and all invitations.

Summary

The forcing notrump is, as indicated in the title of this section, a vital adjunct to any five card major structure. The advantages are many, which may be in a sense the only disadvantage.

For a partnership to play forcing notrump effectively, they must get plenty of practice. Once mastered, it will prove to be a very useful weapon resulting in greatly increased bidding accuracy.

THE NEGATIVE DOUBLE

Playing five card majors, suppose partner opens with one diamond and you hold:

♠ 6 4   ♡ A Q 8 3   ◇ Q 7 2   ♣ Q J 10 3

A perfectly acceptable hand; not strong enough to inaugurate a game forcing sequence but certainly strong enough to explore the possibility of game. Suddenly, right hand opponent overcalls one spade and you have problems. This hand is too strong to pass, but consider the alternative bids. Two hearts? This would imply a five card suit and partner would raise with any three card holding. Two or three diamonds? Partner may hold only a three card suit. Two notrump? Suicidal! Rocky shoals!

Assume the same auction:

North	East	South	West
1 ◇	1 ♠	?	

You are sitting South holding:

♠ 6 3   ♡ Q 10 7 6 5   ◇ A 9 4 3   ♣ Q 3

Again, right hand opponent's overcall creates a problem. With eight high card points, two doubletons and four diamonds, "pass" is a very unappetizing choice. A competitive two diamond call could work out. Opener may hold:

♠ A 7 5   ♡ K 3   ◇ K Q 8 6 5   ♣ J 7 4

or

♠ A Q 5   ♡ K 3   ◇ K Q 8 6 5 2   ♣ A 7

In the first case, he would pass two diamonds; in the second case, he would bid three notrump, solving all your problems. But opener may hold:

♠ 8 7 5 4   ♡ A K 8 2   ◇ J 7 6   ♣ A 5

and again, he would pass. You are now playing this hand in a seven card diamond fit instead of a nine card heart fit.

These problems are all solved in modern bidding by treating a low level double by responder as a takeout for the unbid suits. This type of responder's takeout double is termed "negative" because it is not designed to penalize the opponent. Instead it is an attempt to compete for the right of becoming declarer by discovering your side's best suit holding.

Some rules concerning the negative double:

(1) If right hand opponent overcalls partner's minor with a major, the negative doubler holds at least four cards in the other major.

  (a) If that major is only a four card holding, responder has either length in the fourth suit, support for partner's suit, or stoppers for notrump.

  (b) With five or more cards in hearts after a spade overcall, responder may be single suited, but lack the strength for a bid at the two level.

(2) There is no upper limit regarding high card strength. The negative double is employed whenever a free bid is incorrect, either because of inadequate high cards or awkward distribution.

(3) Useful distribution can be a substitute for high card strength — the negative double allows responder to compete freely.

(4) A negative double is not limited to major suits. After the sequence:

North	East	South	West
1 ♡	1 ♠	?	

a negative double may be employed to show both minor suits.

(5) A partnership must agree on the level at which responder's doubles cease to be negative. This may range from the "traditional" negative double after a one or two spade overcall to the "super scientific" negative double that is applicable no matter what the level. We recommend an agreement that responder's double should be negative through either three spades or four of a minor, while all higher doubles are for penalties. Again, this is a question of partnership agreement. As you become more comfortable with the negative double structure, you may wish to adjust the level. The only thing that should be observed in this context is that the higher the opponents bid, the stronger (or more distributional) the negative doubler's hand should be.

There are very strict rules and regulations for the proper use of the negative double and misuse can lead to disastrous results. The following hands present the general principles of the negative double. In each of these auctions you are seated South.

(1) ♠ 6   ♡ A 9 5 3   ◇ K 9 3   ♣ J 6 5 4 2

North	East	South	West
1 ◇	1 ♠	Dbl	

When the opponents have overcalled in a major suit, if you hold at least four cards in the other major suit you can make a negative double. However, if you have only four cards in the other major, you must have length in the fourth suit or in partner's first bid suit or stoppers in the opponent's suit.

(2) ♠ 9 8   ♡ K J 10 5 3 2   ◇ 9 7 4   ♣ K 2

North	East	South	West
1 ♣	1 ♠	Dbl	Pass
1 NT	Pass	2 ♡	

This sequence utilizes the negative double to show length in hearts without the strength for a free bid on the two level.

(3) ♠ K 7   ♡ A Q 6 5 3   ◇ 6 4   ♣ K 10 8 2

North	East	South	West
1 ◇	1 ♠	2 ♡	

Here a negative double would be inappropriate since responder holds a five card heart suit and sufficient values to bid freely at the two level. The negative double is used to handle awkward situations, not to create complications where none exist.

(4) ♠ A 5 3   ♡ K 10 8 2   ◇ 7   ♣ K J 7 6 2

North	East	South	West
1 ♣	1 ♠	Dbl	

There is a popular misconception that a negative double always shows a weak hand. In fact, there is no upper limit to a negative double. Some hands may be awkward to bid either from the point of view of high cards as in hand (2), or in this case, because of distribution. By utilizing the negative double, responder is able to investigate a possible four-four heart fit. His plan is to cue bid the ace of spades at his next turn. A possible auction is:

North	East	South	West
1 ♣	1 ♠	Dbl	Pass
2 ♡	Pass	2 ♠	

This is a game forcing sequence coupled with slam interest. Notice that the same auction could be used if opener rebid two diamonds. Responder would still cue bid spades and support clubs at his next turn to bid.

(5) ♠ 8 4   ♡ K Q 7 6   ◇ J 9 4 3 2   ♣ 8 3

North	East	South	West
1 ◇	1 ♠	Dbl	

Despite responder's sparse high card holding, this is a perfectly acceptable negative double. Remember, partner has opened the bidding, so your side has approximately half of the high card points. If partner fails to show four hearts, you will return to diamonds. However, if the minor suit holdings are interchanged:

♠ 6 2   ♡ K Q 8 4   ◇ 7 3   ♣ J 7 6 4 2

You should pass the overcall; your high card points are too sparse to encourage partner.

(6) ♠ 8 7 2   ♡ K J 7 3   ◇ 6   ♣ K J 5 4 2

North	East	South	West
1 ♣	1 ♠	Dbl	2 ♠

On the surface, this problem may appear a bit sticky; left hand opponent has now entered the auction. In fact, the problem has become easier. If partner bids three hearts, you should carry on to game despite holding only eight high card points. If partner rebids three clubs, you should raise to four.

The reasons you should take an aggressive position with this hand are:

(a) You have an excellent fit with partner's first bid suit.

(b) Your singleton diamond is a useful asset.

(c) Left hand opponent's two spade call is a good indication that partner is short in spades.

(7) ♠ K 10 8 6 4   ♡ 7 3   ◇ A 5 4 2   ♣ 6 5

North	East	South	West
1 ◇	1 ♡	1 ♠	

A nice adjunct of the negative double is that responder is guaranteeing a five card spade holding with this auction. With only four spades, he would have doubled (negative).

(8) ♠ K J 7 3   ♡ 9 3   ◇ Q J 8   ♣ Q 7 5 3

North	East	South	West
1 ◇	1 ♡	Dbl	

With only four spades the negative double is correct because an immediate one spade bid would show a five card suit. If partner now rebids one spade, raise to two spades. This shows game interest with a minimum range limit raise. With a better hand such as:

♠ K 10 5 4   ♡ A 2   ◇ K J 4   ♣ 6 4 3 2

jump to three spades. Because of the use of the negative double, opener knows that responder holds exactly four spades. A similar forward-going action would be appropriate after any other rebid — if opener rebids one notrump, raise to two; if opener rebids diamonds, raise to three; if opener bids clubs, rebid notrump.

(9) ♠ 7 3   ♡ 8 2   ◇ Q 9 4 3   ♣ K J 8 6 2

North	East	South	West
1 ♡	1 ♠	Dbl	

Do not let this underaverage high card holding depress you into passing. Again, keep in mind that partner opened the bidding and if he holds four cards (or even three) in either minor, you have first rate competitive chances.

(10) ♠ A Q 10 5 3   ♡ 8   ◇ A 9 6 3   ♣ Q 7 3

North	East	South	West
1 ♡	1 ♠	Pass	

Holding this hand, it would be nice not to be playing negative doubles; one spade is not likely to be a success story for your opponents. This hand will take care of itself, as we will see later. For the time being, sheath your fangs and pass quietly.

In each of the following five problems, you have opened the bidding. With no guidelines except the auction and your imagination, make the appropriate bid in response to partner's negative double. (Assume that your agreement is to use negative doubles through four of a minor).

(1) ♠ A Q 8 4   ♡ 9 3   ◇ A 8 6 4   ♣ A 3 2

North	East	South	West
1 ◇	3 ♡	Dbl	Pass
?			

Four spades. Although your hand is minimum range, responder must hold near opening bid values for a negative double at the three level. A three spade bid may give partner an impossible decision. We admit that you hold only fourteen points, but you do have three quick tricks and a doubleton. In the long run, the aggressive leap to game will be the winning call, but don't be terribly disappointed if this contract goes down.

(2) ♠ 6 5 4 3   ♡ A Q 7 3   ◇ 8   ♣ A K J 6

North	East	South	West
1 ♣	1 ♠	Dbl	2 ♠
?			

Four hearts. Your holding has definitely been improved by the auction. Considering that both opponents have bid spades, responder should hold no more than a singleton and may well be void in that suit. That information, plus your singleton diamond, makes this a first-rate playing hand. If responder makes any effort to move towards slam, you should accept with alacrity. All of your cards are hard-working.

(3) ♠ A 7 4 3 2   ♡ Q 9 5 2   ◇ A K 8   ♣ 7

North	East	South	West
1 ♠	2 ◇	Dbl	Pass
?			

Three hearts. Even though responder was incapable of making a free bid of two hearts, we would not quarrel with an aggressive jump to four hearts. Your assets, however, are such that three hearts should not be in danger and four hearts will be an "iffy" contract if responder is minimum. With a fair holding such as:

♠ 9 8   ♡ K J 10 6 4 3   ◇ Q 4   ♣ Q 6 5

partner should accept the invitation. True, a trump lead might defeat four hearts if hearts break 3-1 (unless the spade suit divides evenly). Nonetheless, the bonus for bidding this type of close game should not be missed.

(4) ♠ K 8   ♡ 8 7   ◊ A 7 4   ♣ A K Q J 3 2

North	East	South	West
1 ♣	1 ♠	Dbl	Pass
?			

Three notrump. A call that puts a lot of pressure on the defense. Don't worry about your doubleton heart; partner has promised heart length with his negative double. This bid could produce a spectacular success. Partner may hold a minimum negative double such as:

♠ 9 6 5   ♡ Q 10 5 4   ◊ K J 8 6   ♣ 10 5

A heart lead, followed by a spade through your king will certainly scuttle three notrump, but against the more likely spade lead, nine tricks will appear as if by magic.

Further Evaluation Of Rebids After A Negative Double

As in any other type of auction, negative double sequences pose two questions: Which suit to play and at what level?

The opening bidder should reevaluate his hand after the negative double to determine whether to make a minimum rebid or take more aggressive action. Three factors add to opener's values:

(a) High card points. A minimum opening is between 12 and 15 high card points. More than 15 points would be a plus factor.

(b) Shape. Length in the negative doubler's implied suit is another plus factor. Thus with:

♠ 7 6   ♡ A Q 5 3   ◊ A Q 9 6   ♣ Q 8 7

and the bidding goes:

North	East	South	West
1 ◊	1 ♠	Dbl	Pass

your hand has improved by virtue of the known 4-4 heart fit.

(c) Shortness in the opponent's suit. A singleton or void in the overcaller's suit is a definite plus. Holding:

♠ K Q 6 4   ♡ A 8 7 3 2   ◊ A Q 2   ♣ 6

North	East	South	West
1 ♡	2 ♣	Dbl*	Pass

*Shows spades

Your singleton club gains in value because the defenders will hold wasted high card points in the club suit.

With better than a minimum opening and support for responder's "known" suit, it is appropriate to jump, telling partner that
the auction has improved your hand. Similarly, with a healthy minimum and support for responder's suit plus a singleton or void in
the overcaller's suit, it is again normally correct to jump. With a fit
in partner's suit plus both of the above advantages (extra high card
points and shortness in overcaller's suit), the opener should cue bid
the overcaller's suit. (This creates a game forcing auction.)

Now try your luck at evaluating the following rebid problems.
(Look at the number of plus values in each hand.) You are South in
each case.

(1) ♠ K 4   ♡ A Q 4 2   ◇ K J 9 6   ♣ J 5 3

South	West	North	East
1 ◇	1 ♠	Dbl	Pass
?			

Two hearts. You have a 4-4 heart fit, but your hand contains no
other plus values; your king of spades has lost its value. This is a
minimum opening bid with no especially attractive distributional
factors. Some strong encouragement by responder is necessary for
you to consider game.

(2) ♠ 7   ♡ K Q 7 6   ◇ A K 9 8 4   ♣ A Q 7

South	West	North	East
1 ◇	1 ♠	Dbl	Pass
?			

Two spades. This hand is a powerhouse in the light of the bidding.
You have an established trump suit (hearts), shortness in the overcaller's suit and excellent high card strength. Let partner know this
by making a game forcing cue bid.

(3) ♠ —   ♡ A K 9 3 2   ◇ A K J 7 4   ♣ K 6 5

South	West	North	East
1 ♡	1 ♠	Dbl	3 ♠
?			

Four spades. Despite the opponents' preemptive attempts, nothing
should deter you from announcing the strength of your hand. None
of responder's rebids can hurt you. If he bids five clubs, show your
diamond suit. (It is close whether you should do so at the five level
or six level). Right hand opponent's three spade jump was an at-

tempt to cut off lines of communication but, by cue bidding at the four level, you have used his bid to your own advantage.

(4) ♠ K 10 9 5   ♡ 6 4   ◇ A 7 3   ♣ K Q J 6

South	West	North	East
1 ♣	1 ♠	Dbl	Pass
?			

One notrump. Simple and straightforward. This is a minimum range hand with two spade stoppers and no support for partner's suits. Unless responder cue bids or raises notrump, there is no chance for game with this hand.

(5) ♠ K 10 9 8   ♡ 8 3   ◇ A K J 4   ♣ A K J

South	West	North	East
1 ◇	1 ♠	Dbl	Pass
?			

Two notrump. Since you intended to rebid two notrump over a one heart response by partner, there is no reason not to do so despite the overcall. Spades are well taken care of and there is no need to worry about the doubleton heart since responder has promised heart length with the negative double.

* * * * * * * *

In olden days, bridge was a much simpler game. With a lot of picture cards and aces, we made a lot of bids. Without high cards, we passed a lot. In this super scientific age, things are not so simple and even "pass" can become very significant. Consider the following sequence:

North	East	South	West
1 ♡	2 ♠	Pass	Pass

You are holding:

♠ 6   ♡ K Q 10 5 2   ◇ A Q 7   ♣ K 7 6 4

Partner may not hold enough values to enter the bidding or he may hold a hand such as:

♠ K Q 10 5 3   ♡ 3   ◇ J 8 6 4   ♣ A 9 2

where he would dearly love to defend two spades doubled. However, since your partnership has agreed to play negative doubles, he cannot double two spades for penalties. This state of affairs creates an obligation for opener to make a special effort to keep the auction open; unless he holds a highly distributional hand, it is usually correct to reopen with a double. In the above example, responder would gratefully convert partner's reopening double to penalties by passing. Under modern bidding methods, it is not necessary to hold extra values for a reopening double.

As a general guideline, reopen with a double whenever you would have been content to pass partner's penalty double. Don't worry about your own shortness in trumps. However, if you don't want partner to make a "penalty pass," reopen with a rebid of your original suit or a new suit, depending on your distribution. For instance, if you hold:

♠ 7   ♡ K 9 7 6 4 2   ◇ 8   ♣ A K J 3 2

and the auction goes:

South	West	North	East
1 ♡	1 ♠	Pass	Pass
?			

a reopening double would be inappropriate because one of the reasons you opened the bidding is your six-five distribution. Bid two clubs.

Occasionally, it is correct not to reopen, mainly when you hold the opposing suit. As an example, suppose you have:

♠ 8 3 2   ♡ K Q 10 3 2   ◇ K J   ♣ A Q 7

North	East	South	West
—	—	1 ♡	2 ♣
Pass	Pass	?	

With six high card points in clubs, it is very unlikely that partner has any desire to penalize two clubs. In addition, he was unable to either make a negative double or raise hearts. All signs point to this hand belonging to the opponents and as such, you should go quietly.

A judicious pass can often reap subtle rewards, especially for the duplicate bridge player. Consider the following situation:

♠ K 10 9 7 6   ♡ 7   ◇ A K Q 3   ♣ K J 10

North	East	South	West
Pass	Pass	1 ♠	2 ♣
Pass	Pass	?	

With this healthy opening bid, you are strongly tempted to do something and not let this auction languish at two clubs, despite your badly placed club honors. North's pass tells an eloquent story, though. He could not make a negative double or support spades, so he must have a very weak hand. In addition, there is a strong likelihood that East-West have a massive combined heart fit and they are probably in the wrong contract. Reopening this auction is more likely to help the opponents locate their heart fit than to produce a plus score for your side.

With this information, test your reopening acumen on the following five hands:

(1) ♠ A Q 6 3 2   ♡ 8   ◇ A 7 4 2   ♣ A 9 3

North	East	South	West
1 ♠	2 ♡	Pass	Pass
?			

Double. It is improbable that partner has nothing since the auction died at the two level. He might be holding a scattered six or seven high card points:

♠ J 5   ♡ J 7 4 3   ◇ K 9 6   ♣ Q 7 4 2

in which case he should return to two spades. Or he may be looking at a solid penalty double of two hearts:

♠ 5   ♡ A Q 9 7 4   ◇ K 9 6   ♣ J 10 7 4

in which case he would, of course, pass the reopening double for penalties. Don't let the singleton heart scare you. With 3½ quick tricks, you should be delighted if partner chooses to defend.

(2) ♠ K J 4   ♡ A 7 6 4 2   ◇ Q J 8   ♣ K 9

North	East	South	West
1 ♡	1 ♠	Pass	Pass
?			

Pass. When you hold king-jack third of opponents' trump suit, it is highly unlikely that partner can pass for penalties. His failure to enter the bidding strongly suggests sparse values, inappropriate distribution, or both. A reopening bid of one notrump should show extra values and would be an overbid with this sort of minimum range hand. The disciplined pass averts potential disaster and respects partner's inability to compete.

(3) ♠ 9   ♡ A 7 3   ◇ A K Q 10 8 6 4   ♣ Q 3

North	East	South	West
1 ◇	1 ♠	Pass	Pass
?			

Three diamonds. Partner may hold excellent spade values, but your hand simply is not suited for defense. A jump in your first bid suit shows length and solidity and is strongly invitational to three notrump.

(4) ♠ K 10 7 3 2   ♡ A Q   ◇ Q 9   ♣ K J 8 3

North	East	South	West
1 ♠	2 ♣	Pass	Pass
?			

Pass. As with hand (2), there is a strong suspicion that partner is looking at next to nothing; your club holding is a good indication that partner is not waiting to penalize East's contract. There is another interesting point about this hand; partner's failure to use a negative double should make opener suspicious that East-West have an eight card heart fit. If this is the case, the opponents are in their worst contract. Why disturb them?

(5) ♠ K Q 7 4 2   ♡ A Q 9 8 6   ◇ Q 3 2   ♣ —

North	East	South	West
1 ♠	2 ♣	Pass	Pass
?			

Two hearts. A reopening double would be inappropriate because much of the value of this hand is its distribution. Get this message across to partner by introducing your second suit. Subsequent rounds of bidding will now prove easier. For example, if the opponents compete to three clubs and partner doubles, you can pass with complete confidence because you have already warned partner that your hand is not suitable for defense.

Summary

The manifold complexities and subtleties of the negative double are one of the major arguments against it. As with the forcing notrump, the negative double must be studied carefully. When in doubt, remember:

(a) The negative double is used to solve awkward bidding problems based either on inadequate high card strength or awkward distribution.

(b) A negative double of a major suit overcall guarantees at least four cards in the other major.

(c) A partnership must agree as to the top level of the negative double.

THE RESPONSIVE DOUBLE
(Optional)

The responsive double, like the negative double, can be used in competitive auctions to handle awkward bidding situations. There are great similarities between negative and responsive doubles, but there are also critical differences. If you are going to employ this useful convention, it is very important to understand the underlying theory.

The two main responsive double rules are:

(a) By opener's side, the responsive double is used by the opening bidder.

(b) By overcaller's side, the responsive double is used by the overcaller's partner.

As with the negative double, your partnership must agree how high to play this convention. However, if you are not yet confident with negative doubles, our recommendation is to master them first.

Consider the following common bidding sequence. You hold:

♠ K J 8	♡ 7 3	◇ K 10 5 4	♣ Q 4 3 2
North	**East**	**South**	**West**
—	1 ♡	Dbl	2 ♡
?			

With nine high card points, it is incumbent for you to compete, but what to bid? Three of a minor? Partner may be 4-3 in the minors and you may pick the wrong one. Two spades on a three card suit? Exotic, especially if South also holds three spades. So let's permit North to double, asking partner to bid.

Two points remain constant throughout any discussion of responsive doubles:

(a) The double is responsive if and only if the opponents have bid the same suit. Thus,

North	East	South	West
—	1 ♡	Dbl	2 ♡
Dbl			

is responsive, while

North	East	South	West
—	1 ♡	Dbl	2 ◇
Dbl			

is penalty oriented.

(b) If the opponents bid one major and you hold four or more cards in the opposite major, bid that suit. Thus, holding:

♠ K J 8 2   ♡ 7 3   ◇ K 10 5 4   ♣ Q 4 3

bid two spades if the auction goes:

North	East	South	West
1 ♡	Dbl	2 ♡	?

The responsive double is only used to solve awkward bidding problems; holding four spades, you have an easy two spade bid.

Examine the following auction which contains both a negative double and a responsive double. This is the South hand:

♠ A Q 7 5 4   ♡ K 8 5   ◇ A 5 4 3   ♣ 9

North	East	South	West
—	—	1 ♠	2 ♣
Dbl	3 ♣	Dbl	

North's double of West's two club overcall is of course negative, showing hearts, while South's double of three clubs is responsive. Both bids are for takeout, showing a desire to compete. Let's take a look at some of the interesting features of this auction.

(a) East-West have bid and supported the same suit. (If the auction had proceeded:

North	East	South	West
—	—	1 ♠	2 ♣
Dbl	3 ◇	Dbl	

South's double would have been a business double since East mentioned a new suit rather than supporting West's suit.)

(b) The opening bidder is the doubler. Negative doubles are employed by responder; responsive doubles are used by the opener.

(c) South does not hold a four card heart suit. If he held four hearts, there would not be a bidding problem.

(d) The responsive doubler's hand should contain either extra values or shortness in the enemy suit. Notice that to the extent that East-West hold high cards in the club suit, South's singleton club becomes an effective tool.

Another use of the responsive double is after an overcall by partner. Examine the following sequence. You (North) hold:

♠ 7 5 3 ♡ Q 7 ◊ K J 10 7 ♣ Q 10 9 7

North	East	South	West
Pass	1 ♠	2 ♡	2 ♠
Dbl			

Your double of two spades is responsive, requesting partner to compete.

(a) When the responsive double is used in an overcall sequence, the responder is always the responsive doubler. Note the difference between this and responsive double situations related to opening bids.

(b) You have support for both unbid suits. Ideally, as in this case, the responsive doubler has sufficient high card strength to justify competing for the hand.*

(c) Ideally, though not mandatory, the responsive doubler should have little in the opponents' trump suit. Change the hand to:

♠ K J 3 ♡ Q 7 ◊ 10 7 3 2 ♣ Q 10 7 3

and the responsive double would be less likely to produce a success, since it may induce partner to compete too eagerly.

*Eight high card points or an especially shapely seven high card points are sufficient.

Now try your hand at the following situations. Examine the hands, examine the auctions, and come up with the winning action.

(1) ♠ 5 4 ♡ K Q 10 9 7 ◇ A Q 10 4 ♣ K 7

North	East	South	West
—	Pass	1 ♡	1 ♠
2 ♡	3 ◇	?	

Double. This is a business double, not a responsive double. The responsive double only applies when both opponents have bid the same suit. Letting partner know you can defend three diamonds may lead to a very profitable situation. North's two heart raise may look like:

♠ K J 10 8 ♡ J 3 2 ◇ 5 4 ♣ A 8 6 5

in which case three diamonds doubled will be a likely massacre and partner will know what to do if West runs to three spades.

(2) ♠ K Q 10 4 ♡ 3 2 ◇ Q 10 7 2 ♣ J 10 2

South	West	North	East
—	1 ♣	2 ♡	2 ♠
?			

Pass. A responsive double is an error with this type of hand. The best chance for a plus score is to defend two spades. If partner reopens with a double, pass for penalties. If he bids three clubs, three notrump should be considered.

Each time you adopt a new convention, you lose something — this time the ability to double two spades.

(3) ♠ A Q 10 7 4 ♡ A Q 10 7 ◇ K 4 3 ♣ 2

North	East	South	West
—	—	1 ♠	2 ♣
Dbl	3 ♣	?	

Four hearts. A responsive double could only serve to muddy the waters. With only three hearts, the responsive double would be appropriate. With four hearts, bid your proven eight card fit. The extra values justify a leap to game rather than a mere three heart call. There should be good chances for game even opposite minimal values.

(4) ♠ K J 10 9 8   ♡ 7 4 3   ◇ A Q J 5   ♣ A

North	East	South	West
—	—	1 ♠	2 ♣
Dbl	3 ♣	?	

Double. A classic responsive double. If partner bids three diamonds, cue bid your ace of clubs as a game try — he can then either sign off at four diamonds or go to game, depending on the strength of his hand. If he bids three hearts, showing five or more hearts, and less than a free response, pass. (Don't be surprised if he takes ten tricks, anyway.)

(5) ♠ 3   ♡ A 5 3   ◇ A K Q 9 7   ♣ K 10 7 4

North	East	South	West
Pass	Pass	1 ◇	1 ♠
Dbl	2 ♠	?	

Double. Again, this is a responsive double. If partner bids hearts, raise to game. As with the previous example, he should be holding five or more hearts since he knows that you do not hold four. (Or else he has support for diamonds or a biddable club suit.)

(6) ♠ K 2   ♡ A K J 5 3 2   ◇ —   ♣ K 10 7 5 4

North	East	South	West
—	—	1 ♡	1 ♠
Dbl	2 ♠		

Four clubs. Responsive doubles should only be used in awkward bidding situations. Since you want to play this hand in either clubs or hearts, bid naturally. We cannot stress too strongly the dangers of misusing a convention. As an example, assume you elected a responsive double. The auction might well proceed:

North	East	South	West
—	—	1 ♡	1 ♠
Dbl	2 ♠	Dbl (?)	3 ♠
5 ◇	Pass	?	

and you are in a great deal of trouble.

Reacting to a responsive double follows the general rules of bridge logic. With a minimum strength hand, clarify your distribution; with extra values, jump the bidding. With a sensational hand, you should cue bid the opponents' suit. The following hands illustrate possible reactions to a responsive double. You are seated South.

(1) ♠ 7 6 5   ♡ A 7 3 2   ◊ 3 2   ♣ K J 3 2

North	East	South	West
1 ◊	1 ♠	Dbl	2 ♠
Dbl	Pass	?	

Bid three clubs. If partner held four hearts, he would bid them. Since the auction makes it almost certain that he does not hold more than two spades, an eight card club fit is a virtual sure thing.

(2) ♠ A J 10 9   ♡ J 9 8 7   ◊ K 3 2   ♣ 8 4

North	East	South	West
1 ♣	1 ♠	Dbl	2 ♠
Dbl	Pass	?	

Pass. Although North's double is for takeout, you should convert this to penalties based on your excellent spade holding. Your side is unlikely to hold an eight card fit and there are sufficient high card resources to expect a two or three trick set.

(3) ♠ A K J 8 7   ♡ 7 4   ◊ K 3   ♣ Q 9 8 6

North	East	South	West
—	1 ♡	1 ♠	2 ♡
Dbl	Pass	?	

Three clubs. Suppress the temptation to rebid your spades. Partner has promised support for the unbid suits and the chance of playing an eight card fit should not be missed. North might be looking at:

♠ 2   ♡ J 3 2   ◊ Q 9 8 7 5   ♣ A 10 5 3

in which case both your score and partnership bidding confidence would suffer from a spade rebid.

(4) ♠ A J 5 4   ♡ 3   ◊ A 7 6 4   ♣ K J 10 3

North	East	South	West
1 ◊	1 ♡	Dbl	3 ♡
Dbl	Pass	?	

Four hearts. West's three heart bid is clearly preemptive, based on distribution, but you are much too strong to be either frightened or preempted. Get this across to partner by cue bidding their suit.

(5) ♠ —   ♡ A 8   ◊ A 10 7 5 3   ♣ Q 9 6 5 4 2

North	East	South	West
1 ♡	1 ♠	Dbl	4 ♠
Dbl	Pass	?	

Five spades. Here the question is how high the partnership has agreed to play responsive doubles. If the double was meant as responsive, you suddenly have a whale of a hand. The opponents are likely to have the vast majority of their high card points in spades which, of course, will be useless on defense against a suit contract. Tell this to partner by cue bidding five spades, requesting him to bid a minor suit slam. Even if partner means the double for penalties, you should bid five clubs.

(6) ♠ A 9 4 3   ♡ 7   ◊ K J 7 2   ♣ J 8 6 4

North	East	South	West
1 ♡	2 ◊	Dbl	3 ◊
Dbl	Pass	?	

Pass. The responsive double helps clarify the situation. Since opener does not hold four spades, it is pretty easy to guess at his hand pattern, assisted by the enemy interference. Three spades, five hearts, one diamond and four clubs. Since empathizing with partner is winning technique, let's empathize. Opener did not show his club suit because:

(a) He did not want to go past a possible three notrump contract and;

(b) He wanted to show tolerance for spades in case you held a five card suit.

With nine high card points and diamond values opposite shortness (which is a duplication in values), game is not likely for your side. However, a singleton in partner's first bid suit is a superior defensive value; a conversion of partner's responsive double to penalties rates to be the winning bid. Please notice that with the difficulties in communication, three notrump should be anywhere from extremely difficult to downright unmanageable.

TWO OVER ONE FORCING

One of the first rules of basic bidding is that a two over one response to partner's opening bid promises at least ten points and is both forcing for one round and normally promises another bid.

As a modification to this rule, most modern experts have agreed to treat a two over one as a virtual game force. The great advantage of this agreement is that after a two over one response, neither side has to worry about a "surprise pass" below the game level.

The following guidelines cover the salient features of the two over one game forcing agreement.

(1) After a two over one response, the partnership is committed to keep the bidding open until at least the game level. (The only exception to this is Rule 2.)

(2) The game forcing response shows only "invitational" values when responder first bids a minor on the two level and then rebids the same minor at the three level. As an example, the following sequences show

    (a) Nine to twelve high card points

    (b) No fit for opener's suit(s)

    (c) A concentration of values in the indicated minor.

North	South		North	South
1 ♠	2 ♣	or	1 ♡	2 ♢
2 NT	3 ♣		3 ♣	3 ♢

(3) After a game force has been established, the general rule is "the slower the auction, the greater the hand." To illustrate this principle, consider the following hand:

♠ 10 7 4   ♡ A 4   ◇ A Q 10 9 7 6   ♣ Q 2

Partner opens the bidding with one spade. You have sufficient strength to establish a game force, so two diamonds is the obvious response. Opener rebids two spades. With this hand, your rebid should be a direct jump to four spades, letting partner know that you have little beyond your original game force.

Now let's improve the hand by adding the king of spades:

♠ K 10 7   ♡ A 4   ◇ A Q 10 9 7 6   ♣ Q 2

North	South
1 ♠	2 ◇
2 ♠	?

Now you hold extra values and the correct bid is three spades.

The logic is simply that since a game force has been established, keeping the auction lower leaves more room for slam exploration. The following auctions illustrate the two over one principles in action.

(1) ♠ J 2   ♡ J 5 4 3   ◇ 2   ♣ A K Q 10 9 7

North	South
1 ♠	2 ♣
2 ◇	3 ♣
3 NT	Pass

South's rebid of three clubs turns the game force into an invitational sequence, showing good clubs with little outside values. From South's point of view, North's two diamond rebid is quite discouraging; if North had rebid two hearts, South's hand would have improved dramatically and would be worth a four heart bid. Even a two spade rebid, showing a sixth spade, would be encouraging. South might well fall in love with his singleton diamond and try for a spade game. When North bids three notrump, South, with a potential six tricks to contribute to the cause, has no problem passing.

(2) ♠ A K 9 7 5 4 3   ♡ A Q 8 4   ◇ —   ♣ 9 7

North	South
—	1 ♠
2 ♡	3 ♡
4 ♡	4 ♠
5 ♣	7 ♡

90

North's two heart response was a pleasant surprise, showing at least five hearts and an opening bid. South indicated slam interest by raising to three hearts. (A jump to four hearts would deny slam interest). With nothing to spare, North retreated to four hearts. South felt his hand was worth one more try and cue bid his ace of spades. North cue bid the ace of clubs, which was just what the doctor ordered. North's hand:

♠ 6   ♡ K J 10 9 2   ◇ J 5 4   ♣ A K J 6

Declarer easily established the spades to bring home the grand slam. Please notice the simplicity of the auction based on the ability to rebid a forward-going three hearts.

(3) ♠ J 4   ♡ K J 7   ◇ A J 9 7 6   ♣ A K 10

North	South
1 ♠	2 ◇
3 NT	Pass

In accord with our general theme of using minimum bids to show good hands, North's three notrump rebid denies extra values. This makes South's rebid decision easy — opposite a minimum opening bid, slam would be very iffy. Rather than risk a possible negative score, South passes and takes the sure plus.

Since a two notrump rebid by opener would be forcing, it is reserved for better hands, permitting the partnership to exchange information at the lowest possible level. Be sure to discuss this with your partner, since it is a reversal of former methods, where the jump to three notrump showed a very good hand (a notrump opening with a five card major in most cases) and the two notrump rebid showed minimum values.

(4) ♠ Q 7 2   ♡ 4   ◇ A Q J 5 4   ♣ K Q 10 3

North	South
1 ♠	2 ◇
2 ♡	3 ♣
3 ◇	3 ♠

Observe how neatly the "we-can't-pass-under-game" rule works here. South's auction paints a clear picture of a hand of 3-1-5-4 distribution with slam interest.

This would be a poor use of the splinter bid, since South holds only three trumps. The diamond suit plus the heart shortage are both important when considering slam and these features must both be communicated to partner. Since he needs both two aces and good spades, he must make the final decision.

(5) ♠ Q 3   ♡ K J 5 4   ◇ 3   ♣ A K 10 9 5 2

North	South
1 ♠	2 ♣
2 ♡	4 ◇ !

This is a situation where it is possible to have one's cake and eat it too. Since three diamonds would have been natural and forcing, South reckoned that four diamonds would be a splinter bid. Thus, in two bids, South describes a hand containing game forcing values, a good club suit, four card heart support, and a singleton diamond. If South feared a misunderstanding, he could have bid three hearts, but four diamonds is much more eloquent.

Since responder cannot pass opener's rebid in a two over one auction, a special meaning has become attached to a jump rebid in the same suit by opener. It shows a solid suit, but not necessarily more than a minimum opening bid. With a solid six card suit, the high card range might be from 13 up; with a solid seven card suit, the hand might contain as few as the 11 high card points required for an opening bid. Once again, be sure that your partner is on the same wave length as you are when using this bid.

Summary

The two over one game force can be incorporated into any bidding structure and is an agreement that will make for happier partnerships.

Since minimum holdings are shown with the forcing notrump response, it is unlikely that you will get overboard very often. The advantage of being able to explore a hand slowly without having to worry about being passed out in a partial is more than sufficient reason to adopt this bidding philosophy.

The next section on temporizing sequences by responder will further analyze this subject.

TEMPORIZING SEQUENCES BY RESPONDER

After a major suit opening bid, responder has numerous choices how to conduct the auction based on the shape and quality of his hand. With a good hand and trump support, responder can employ a limit raise or a forcing raise. With a poor hand, responder can raise partner's suit one level with three or more trumps or employ the forcing notrump (see page 52) in an effort to find a suitable landing spot.

However, there are two situations where responder should not support partner's suit directly even though he holds game forcing values.

(a) If responder holds adequate trump support but the trump support is not the prime feature of his hand.

(b) With sparse or non-existent support for partner's major suit.

Hands With Adequate Trump Support

Assume partner opens the bidding with one of a major and you hold game going values plus a long suit headed by top honors, in addition to trump support. As an example, partner opens with one spade and you hold:

♠ K 6 5 ♡ A K Q J 7 3 ◇ 8 7 ♣ 6 5

You are certain of an eight card spade fit and wish to force to game. A direct raise of partner's suit would not do justice to the trick-taking potential of this hand. A two heart bid is the correct call, planning to support partner's spades with the next available rebid.

The following five hands contain game going values opposite an opening bid. What response best describes the prime feature of the hand?

93

(1) ♠ 6　♡ Q 10 8 3　◊ A K 7 6 4 3　♣ K 3
(Your partner opens with one heart.)

Two diamonds. After partner's one heart opening bid, you have delightful choices — what bid gives partner the most information? With the singleton spade, a direct forcing raise of three notrump would certainly be incorrect, so the choices are between a three spade splinter bid and the two diamond call to show a good long suit. We opt for the two diamond call since possibilities of slam revolve around partner's holding in diamonds, plus his outside controls. (We cannot repeat often enough that whenever game is assured, the possibility of slam should always come to mind.) The splinter bid crowds the auction; you would never be able to communicate possession of a powerful six card suit to partner. It also points out to the opponents that they possess most of the spade suit.

(2) ♠ K J 8 3　♡ 7 6　◊ A Q 6 5 3　♣ K 4
(Your partner opens with one spade.)

Three notrump. The prime feature of this hand is the excellent trump support and this should be communicated to partner as quickly as possible. The five card diamond suit is a shade too weak to be treated as a real asset unless your three notrump response is sufficient for opener to show slam interest.

(3) ♠ A 8 6 5 4　♡ 9　◊ A K J 3　♣ 4 3 2
(Your partner opens with one spade.)

Four hearts. This is a superb responding hand. With five trumps and a useful ruffing value, a splinter bid is the quickest way to get this message across. The texture of your diamond suit holding is excellent but with only four cards this is not a "long suit" source of tricks. Again, opener must become excited by the singleton heart for responder to have visions of slam.

(4) ♠ 6 5 4　♡ K 8 7 3 2　◊ —　♣ A K 9 3 2
(Your partner opens with one heart.)

Two clubs. Although responder holds only ten high card points, the fifth trump plus a void in diamonds makes this hand more than sufficient for a game force. If opener can control spades, slam is a real consideration. Let opener know about the good side suit; it will help the subsequent decision making process.

(5) ♠ 6 5 4 ♡ K 8 7 3 2 ◇ — ♣ A K 9 3 2
     (Your partner opens with one spade.)

Two hearts. Show the major suit first, planning to bid clubs and then support spades, indicating a shortage in diamonds. Once again, despite the minimum number of high card points, there should be a game in one of your three suits.

(6) ♠ 8 7 5 ♡ A K 6 3 ◇ K Q 8 5 3 ♣ 9
     (Your partner opens with one heart.)

Four clubs. Although a two diamond bid is certainly a consideration, the suit is a bit too ragged to be considered the prime feature of this hand.

The following hands are taken from actual play; let's explore the evolution of each auction.

(1)   **North**
                       ♠ A 7 5 3 2
                       ♡ 8
                       ◇ A K J 5
                       ♣ 9 5 2

                       South
                       ♠ K Q J 9 8
                       ♡ K J 9
                       ◇ 8 4
                       ♣ A J 8

South	North
1 ♠	4 ♡
4 ♠	Pass

A single, straightforward splinter auction. Despite a healthy opening bid, South realized that his hearts were not an asset for slam purposes and subsided in four spades, which produced precisely ten tricks after a club lead. (Interestingly enough, this hand occurred in a team match and the optimistic bidders at the other table reached five spades, going set one trick.)

(2)

North
♠ 7
♡ Q 10 7 4
◇ A K 8 5 4 3
♣ K 4

South
♠ 6 4 3
♡ A K J 5 3 2
◇ 7 6
♣ A 5

South	North
1 ♡	2 ◇
2 ♡	3 ♡
4 ♣	4 ◇
4 ♡	6 ♡
Pass	

Responder's rebid is the key call of this auction. Since the immediate two diamond response created a virtual game forcing sequence, his rebid of three hearts shows a stronger hand than a jump to four hearts. A jump to four hearts would have said, "I have good diamonds and trump support but nothing else." Despite holding only twelve high card points, South respected responder's desire to explore for slam by cue bidding the ace of clubs. North cue bid the ace of diamonds, and since this did not show extra values, South signed off at four hearts. North felt that his second round control in spades warranted a leap to slam.

(3)

North
- ♠ K J 9 6
- ♡ 3 2
- ◊ A Q
- ♣ K 9 5 4 2

South
- ♠ A Q 8 5 3
- ♡ Q 9
- ◊ K 7
- ♣ A Q 10 8

South	North
1 ♠	3 NT
4 ♣	4 ◊
4 NT	5 ♣
5 ◊	5 ♠
Pass	

It often takes as much skill to stay out of a bad slam as it does to reach a good one. The above subtle auction bears close study. After responder's game forcing three notrump bid, opener cue bid the ace of clubs. Responder, who certainly had nothing to be ashamed of, cue bid his ace of diamonds. Opener's four notrump bid is emphatically not Blackwood. Whenever a cue bidding sequence has begun, four notrump is a temporizing call requesting information.* Being an obedient partner responder showed the king of clubs while opener countered by showing the king of diamonds. With nothing else to say, responder retreated to five spades. Opener knew that if responder held the heart king, he would have bid five hearts. Therefore, he knew that the excellent potential of the combined hands was marred by two quick heart losers. Since West was on lead with the ace-king of hearts, disaster was avoided.

*This is often referred to as "Declarative Interrogative" or D.I. (A silly name for a convention.)
D = Declaring extra values and slam intentions;
I = Inquiring if partner can cue bid further.

(4)

North
♠ 9 8 5
♡ K 9 7 6 3
◇ —
♣ A K 7 5 3

South
♠ A 10 7
♡ A Q 5 4 2
◇ Q 10 3
♣ Q 9

South	North
1 ♡	2 ♣
2 NT	3 ♡
3 ♠	4 ♣
4 ♡	5 ◇
6 ♡ !	Pass

This auction is a good example of partnership trust. Although South's two notrump rebid did not promise extra values, responder's three heart rebid requested further information. South dutifully cue bid his ace of spades and North cue bid his ace of clubs. With nothing further to say, South signed off in four hearts. Feeling his hand was worth one more try, responder cue bid his diamond void. South thought for a while about the auction and determined that he had showed weakness with two of his bids (two notrump and four hearts). Yet, in the face of this, responder had made another slam try. South now decided that his queen of clubs was a very valuable card and leaped to the small slam.

Looking at both hands, a grand slam is an excellent bet, but it was very difficult for North-South to realize the perfect fit.

(5)

North
- ♠ 8 6 3
- ♡ A K 10 4 3
- ◊ K Q 10 4
- ♣ 2

South
- ♠ Q
- ♡ Q 9 7 5 2
- ◊ A 8 7
- ♣ K Q J 10

South	North
1 ♡	4 ♣
4 ♡	Pass

This auction is similar to that of hand (1) with duplicated holdings opposite a singleton. Notice that there are 26 high card points between the two hands, plus potential distributional values, yet slam is not possible. Hand (4) produced slam with only 24 high card points. It is often not a matter of the quantity of high cards but their quality and location.

* * *

The previous hands illustrate the theory of showing the prime assets of a hand — trump support, singletons or long suits. The following hands are rebid problems. What bid will best aid opener's judgment in placing the final contract?

(1) ♠ K 6 5 2   ♡ A K 9 3 2   ◊ Q 8   ♣ 6 4

North	South
1 ♠	2 ♡
2 NT	?

Four spades. Here the decision is between the possibility of slam exploration by making the strong bid of three spades or merely leaping directly to four spades. Three spades would be a shade aggressive; you have already stated that you hold game forcing values by making a two over one response of two hearts at your first turn. There is nothing beyond that in the way of assets; do not bid the same values twice. If partner tries to become ambitious, it must be because of his own extra values and not at your instigation. Four spades states that you have said your all with your initial game forcing bid.

(2) ♠ J 8 3   ♡ K 10 3   ◇ Q 10 5   ♣ A K 6 5

North	South
1 ♣	2 ♣
2 NT	?

Three spades. Since opener's two notrump bid can be made on any of a large range of hands, you should show that your opening bid includes trump support. Any further action is up to partner.

(3) ♠ K 8 6 5 4 2   ♡ K 3   ◇ A J 6 2   ♣ 7

North	South
1 ♡	1 ♠
2 ♡	?

Four hearts. A continued example of pragmatism. You could take a conservative view and bid three hearts (nonforcing though highly invitational since your initial response was not a two over one call), but the important thing to understand is that partner's rebid showed a six card suit. Your singleton club is likely to be helpful in a heart contract; rebidding spades or introducing the diamond suit can only lead to confusion.

(4) ♠ Q 6   ♡ —   ◇ A J 8 5 3   ♣ A K 9 6 4 3

North	South
1 ♠	2 ♣
2 ♠	?

Three diamonds. This hand is too strong to merely raise spades; the three diamond rebid is a reverse showing extra values. If opener should now support one of your minors, a strong attempt should be made to reach a minor suit slam. If opener rebids three notrump, correct to four spades; he will understand that you are very short in hearts.

(5) ♠ 8 3 2   ♡ 7   ◇ A K 6 5 2   ♣ A 9 4 2

North	South
1 ♠	2 ◇
2 NT	?

Four spades. True, this is a good game-going hand, but the weakness of the trump holding is a cause for conservatism. If the spade holding were slightly better — Q 9 8 for example — an exploratory three spade bid would be appropriate.

When a Trump Fit is Sparse or Non-existent

The last type of strong hand to consider is one which contains game forcing values but an inability to support partner's major suit opening bid.

The correct approach is to look for another place to play — the unbid major, notrump or a minor. Matchpoint players tend to avoid minors because of the extra point bonus involved in notrump, but at IMP scoring or rubber bridge the possibility of minor suit games must not be overlooked.

The following five hands are responder's rebid problems. In each case, a game force has been initiated.

(1) ♠ 8 3   ♡ K J 5 2   ◊ A K Q 6 2   ♣ K 4

North	South
1 ♠	2 ◊
2 ♡	?

Three hearts. There are two questions in this auction: Where to play the contract and how high? Opener's two heart rebid is a welcome surprise. Since responder holds 16 prime high card points and a running diamond suit, slam exploration is certainly appropriate. A three heart rebid signals extra values to opener. Similar to previous examples involving support, the jump to four hearts, inhibiting slam exploration, would show a weaker hand.

(2) ♠ A 9 8 7   ♡ 6   ◊ 5 4 3   ♣ A K Q J 5

North	South
1 ♡	2 ♣
2 ◊	?

Two spades. Opener's rebid has not solved any problems and you are still in the exploratory stages of this auction. Notice that you have no fear of the auction dying since your initial two club response insured that game must be reached. Further, the bid of a new suit by responder is always forcing.

(3) ♠ 7 6   ♡ 8 2   ◊ A Q J 8   ♣ A Q J 10 3

North	South
1 ♣	2 ♣
2 ♡	?

Two notrump. With a slightly weaker hand (lacking either of the minor suit queens, for instance), you would close out the bidding with three notrump. Here you have a slightly better than game forcing hand and should give opener as much room as possible to describe his hand.

(4) ♠ 6 5   ♡ Q 7 6   ◊ K Q 10 3 2   ♣ A J 10

North	South
1 ♠	2 ◊
2 ♡	?

Three notrump. Compare this with hand (3). Here you have twelve high card points which is certainly enough to inaugurate a game force opposite partner's opening bid. However, this hand contains no extras. With both minors well stopped, three notrump should more than likely be a successful contract. Partner will pass unless he has either extra values or wild distribution.

(5) ♠ 6 4   ♡ 9 7 3   ◊ A Q J 10 3 2   ♣ K 8

North	South
1 ♠	2 ◊
2 NT	?

Three diamonds, Your original two over one response was ostensibly showing a game going hand. Repeating the minor suit tells partner that you fudged a bit on high card points, but your suit is quite strong. He is permitted to pass your rebid.

Now let's look at both hands for the sequences started above and see how they proceed to a final contract.

(1)

North
- ♠ A Q 7 6 4
- ♡ A Q 6 4
- ◇ 9
- ♣ A 5 3

South
- ♠ 8 3
- ♡ K J 5 2
- ◇ A K Q 6 2
- ♣ K 4

North	South
1 ♠	2 ◇
2 ♡	3 ♡
4 ♣	4 ◇
4 ♠	5 ♣
5 ♡	6 ♡

Three hearts initiated a slam exploratory sequence; South and North then took turns cue bidding their aces. After North's four spade cue bid, South was reasonably certain that a slam in hearts could be made; with poor trumps North might well have attempted to sign off in four hearts rather than cue bidding his ace of spades. If opener also held the king of spades, there might be a grand slam, and with this in mind, South showed his king of clubs. When North failed to cue bid the king of spades, South knew that the grand slam would depend on a finesse at best, and settled for the excellent small slam.

103

(2)

North
- ♠ Q 6 5
- ♡ K Q 8 7 5
- ◇ A Q 8 2
- ♣ 2

South
- ♠ A 9 8 7
- ♡ 6
- ◇ 5 4 3
- ♣ A K Q J 6

North	South
1 ♡	2 ♣
2 ◇	2 ♠
2 NT	3 NT

Although South has a healthy game force, the auction has made clear the fact that no good trump fit exists. With this in mind, South correctly subsides in three notrump. Please notice that responder has described a good hand to partner by bidding spades. In the light of North's lack of interest, further exploration would be inappropriate. Note that the original two club response simplifies the bidding — a sequence of one heart—one spade—two diamonds—three clubs would imply better (or longer) spades.

(3)

North
- ♠ A K 8 4 3
- ♡ A J 7 6
- ◊ 2
- ♣ K 6 4

South
- ♠ 7 6
- ♡ 8 2
- ◊ A Q J 8
- ♣ A Q J 10 3

North	South
1 ♠	2 ♣
2 ♡	2 NT
3 ♣	3 ◊
4 NT	5 ♡
6 ♣	

By rebidding two notrump, responder gives opener a chance to complete the description of his hand by showing delayed club support. Since opener has bid three suits, he must be short in diamonds. South probes for a slam by cue bidding the ace of diamonds. Opener can now bid Blackwood and place the final contract.

(4)

North
- ♠ A K 7 4 3
- ♡ A J 5 2
- ◊ 6
- ♣ K 5 3

South
- ♠ 6 5
- ♡ Q 7 6
- ◊ K Q 10 3 2
- ♣ A J 10

North	South
1 ♠	2 ◊
2 ♡	3 NT

Simple and straightforward. Responder informs partner that he has neither extra values nor a good fit with either of partner's suits. North does not wish to fish in troubled waters and passes.

(5)

North
- ♠ K Q 10 5 3
- ♡ A Q 6
- ◇ 6 5
- ♣ A 10 2

South
- ♠ 6 4
- ♡ 9 7 3
- ◇ A Q J 10 3 2
- ♣ K 8

North	South
1 ♠	2 ◇
2 NT	3 ◇
3 NT	

When South shows a good diamond suit and a hand just short of an opening bid, North's good major suit controls and doubleton diamond cause him to feel that three notrump should be a good bet.

Summary

Treating a two level response to one of a major as a game force is a very useful tool since it keeps auctions relaxed and permits low level slam tries. The general rule: After the partnership is committed to game, the slower the auction, the stronger the hand. Jump support of partner's suit after a two over one response tends to deny extra values, while a simple raise is usually designed to elicit further information. An important fact to remember: Responder shows extra values by reversing or introducing a new suit.

THE FLANNERY CONVENTION

We had mentioned previously the rebid problem when opener has bid one heart with four spades, five hearts and doubletons in both minors and partner has responded with a forcing notrump.

To circumvent this problem, William Flannery of Pittsburgh, Pa., has proposed the use of an artificial two diamond opening to show a minimum range opening bid (11-15 HCPs) containing precisely five hearts and four spades.

Examples of hands that would be appropriate for a Flannery two diamond opening bid are:

(a) ♠ K J 5 4   ♡ A Q 10 7 6   ◇ J 7   ♣ Q 2

(b) ♠ A K J 2   ♡ J 9 8 7 6   ◇ A 7 4   ♣ 3

(c) ♠ A J 9 7   ♡ Q 10 9 8 7   ◇ A 4   ♣ A J

(d) ♠ A K 3 2   ♡ A K 9 4 3   ◇ 3   ♣ J 7 4

(e) ♠ K Q J 10   ♡ K J 10 8 7   ◇ K J 5 4   ♣ —

If opener bids one heart, there is a strong implication that (unless he started with six hearts or a very strong hand), he does not hold four spades. Therefore, responder will not bid one spade unless he is prepared to be supported with three trumps.*

After a one heart opening bid, responder would bid one notrump holding:

♠ K 9 3 2   ♡ J 9   ◇ 8 4 3   ♣ K 10 8 4

and would bid one spade holding:

♠ K J 9 8 2   ♡ J 7   ◇ 8 4   ♣ K 10 8 4

---

*This treatment must be alerted in duplicate games.

Examine the following hands and determine the correct opening bid.

(1) ♠ K J 9 3 ♡ A K Q J 5 ◊ J 3 2 ♣ 9

Two diamonds. With 15 HCPs and excellent texture in both majors, this is a maximum two diamond opening. While we freely admit that the singleton club increases the potential playing value of this hand, partner must have a trump fit for the singleton to be a useful asset.

(2) ♠ A K J 3 ♡ K J 10 8 7 2 ◊ 3 2 ♣ 7

One heart. This hand is inappropriate for a two diamond opening because of the sixth heart. There are some players who have modified Flannery to allow for a four-six distribution. We feel that this further complicates the subsequent auction for a very minor gain.

(3) ♠ K Q 10 3 ♡ A Q 7 5 3 ◊ A J ♣ Q 2

One heart. This hand is too strong for a two diamond opening. You should plan to "reverse" by bidding spades at your next turn.

(4) ♠ Q 5 4 3 ♡ 10 7 4 3 2 ◊ A ♣ A Q 10

Two diamonds. Despite the poor quality of both majors, this hand contains the necessary shape and high card strength to utilize Flannery.

(5) ♠ K Q 5 4 ♡ K J 9 8 4 ◊ J 5 4 2 ♣ —

Pass. With only ten high card points, this hand is too weak to open.

Responding to Flannery

Responses to Flannery may be divided into two areas:

A. Natural Responses
  1. Two hearts or two spades
  2. Three hearts or three spades
  3. Four hearts or four spades
  4. Three clubs or three diamonds
  5. Three notrump
  6. Pass

B. Two Notrump (Artificial)

Natural Responses

The following simple schedule defines the natural responses available after a two diamond opening bid by partner.

1. Two hearts or two spades. A complete denial of any game interest. Opener should not bid again, even with a maximum range hand. For example:

(a) ♠ Q 3 2   ♡ 7   ◊ A Q 9 7 4   ♣ J 9 8 3
Bid two spades.

(b) ♠ 5 3   ♡ Q 7 4   ◊ K Q J 3   ♣ 9 8 4 2
Bid two hearts.

(c) ♠ J 10 8 7   ♡ Q 3   ◊ Q 10 2   ♣ K 7 4 3
Bid two spades.

2. Three hearts or three spades. Invitational, asking opener to decide whether to play for a part score or bid game. Opener should make his decision based on high card points, major suit texture and quick tricks. With good values in two out of three of these areas, he should accept the invitation and bid four of the appropriate major. Examples of an invitational bid:

(a) ♠ K 9 7 6   ♡ Q 6   ◊ Q 7 6   ♣ A 10 7 6
Bid three spades.

(b) ♠ A 5 4   ♡ J 5 3 2   ◊ K 9 6 5   ♣ K 2
Bid three hearts.

(c) ♠ A K 3 2   ♡ Q 2   ◊ 10 8 6 4   ♣ J 7 6
Bid three spades.

3. Four hearts or four spades. These are shut-out bids and opener is required to pass. Examples:

(a) ♠ K Q 10 7   ♡ Q 9   ◊ A 5 3   ♣ Q 9 8 4
Bid four spades.

(b) ♠ 8   ♡ Q 9 7 4   ◊ K Q 10 4   ♣ A 5 4 2
Bid four hearts.

(c) ♠ Q   ♡ A Q 8   ◊ A Q 5 4   ♣ 7 6 3 2
Bid four hearts.

*4. Three clubs or three diamonds. Three of a minor is forcing and shows a hand of opening bid strength with at least five cards in the bid suit and little tolerance for play in the majors. For example:

(a) ♠ A 5   ♡ 7 2   ◇ K 8 5   ♣ A Q 10 9 7 5

Bid three clubs.

(b) ♠ Q 5 2   ♡ A 3   ◇ A J 10 9 7 6   ♣ Q 4

Bid three diamonds.

(c) ♠ A 5   ♡ Q   ◇ J 9 8   ♣ K Q J 10 6 4 3

Bid three clubs.

5. Three notrump. Another shut-out bid showing a healthy opening bid with firm stoppers in the minor suits and no eight card major suit fit. Examples of a three notrump response are:

(a) ♠ K 7 3   ♡ 5 4   ◇ A K 10 4   ♣ K Q 10 3

Bid three notrump.

(b) ♠ 5 4   ♡ J 7   ◇ K J 10   ♣ A K Q J 3 2

Bid three notrump.

(c) ♠ J 5 3   ♡ 3 2   ◇ K J 9 7 3   ♣ A K Q

Bid three notrump.

Let's try a few responding problems. In each case, partner opens the bidding with two diamonds. What is the correct response?

(1) ♠ K 3   ♡ Q 2   ◇ K 7 6 4 2   ♣ J 7 4 3

Two hearts. With this poor hand game is out of the question. A plus score is unlikely against good defense and the 5-2 fit is probably the best landing spot.

(2) ♠ A Q 9 8 5   ♡ 7   ◇ A 7 6 5   ♣ Q 10 3

Four spades. A first rate playing hand. The singleton heart is likely to be an effective value. Don't be surprised at overtricks. An invitational three spades would be much too conservative.

(3) ♠ A 9 8   ♡ 3   ◇ K J 10 9   ♣ K 8 5 4 2

Two spades. Making a virtue of necessity. Although you hold more than a fair share of high card points, there is no eight card major suit fit and three notrump is not likely to be successful because you have no source of tricks.

*See pages 119-120 for other meanings for these bids.

(4) ♠ Q   ♡ J 7   ◇ J 10 9 8   ♣ K 10 8 7 6 4

Two hearts. Don't panic. This hand is a terrible misfit, but any attempt to play clubs will alert the opponents to your problem. Your main hope is that nobody doubles!

(5) ♠ K J 9 3   ♡ A 3 2   ◇ J 10 3   ♣ J 10 8

Three spades. Although this hand is not strong in high cards, the fact that 80% of the points are in hearts and spades make it a first rate game try. In fact, the only other choice is to bid game directly. Please notice that we choose spades rather than hearts since the 4-4 fit is likely to play better than the 5-3 fit.

(6) ♠ A 6 5   ♡ Q   ◇ K J 10 9   ♣ K J 10 8 7

Three notrump. No fit in either major suit is a definite disadvantage but with 14 HCPs and well stopped minor suits, game should be tried.

(7) ♠ K 7   ♡ 8   ◇ A Q J 7 6 5   ♣ K 5 3 2

Three diamonds. This is a forcing bid, signalling partner that while you have no interest in the majors, your hand contains a good suit coupled with enough strength to try for game. Three notrump would be a poor second choice; if opener does not hold a high card in clubs, there will be too much work to do.

Two Notrump (An artificial and exploratory response)

Although the two diamond opening is very informative, it may not provide responder with sufficient information to make an intelligent decision. When responder bids two notrump, he is asking opener to further describe his precise shape and strength. Opener should rebid according to the following schedule:

  (a) Three clubs   = 4-5-1-3 distribution
  (b) Three diamonds = 4-5-3-1 distribution
  (c) Three hearts   = 4-5-2-2 distribution with 11-12 HCPs
  (d) Three spades   = 4-5-2-2 distribution with 14-15 HCPs
  (e) Three notrump   = 4-5-2-2 distribution with stoppers in both minors and 14-15 HCPs
  (f) Four clubs   = 4-5-0-4 distribution
  (g) Four diamonds   = 4-5-4-0 distribution.

Although this is quite a mouthful, these bids are quite logical and should not be difficult to learn. The main thing to remember is that with longer clubs, bid clubs and with longer diamonds, bid diamonds.

Note that neither the three heart nor the three spade bid response allows for thirteen point hands. You must judge whether you hold a thirteen point minimum or a thirteen point maximum. Clues to look for are the texture of the major suits, number of taking tricks (an ace is better than two queens, a king is better than an unsupported queen and jack, number of ten spots, etc.) . . . use your judgment!

The following hands are rebid problems. In response to your two diamond (Flannery) opening bid, partner "popped the question" by bidding two notrump. Make the appropriate bid using the response schedule as a reference.

(1) ♠ A Q 10 4   ♡ A K 10 9 7   ◇ 6 4   ♣ 4 3

Three spades. Your choices are clearly between three hearts (minimum) and three spades (maximum). Concentrated values in the majors are a big plus. Partner is investigating the possibility of game; with this good hand, choose the encouraging response.

(2) ♠ K Q J 10   ♡ A K Q 5 4   ◇ 7 6 5   ♣ 3

Three diamonds. With this super-maximum, you are quite happy to receive encouragement from partner, but for the moment, tell him your minor suit length.

(3) ♠ K 8 6 4   ♡ K J 4 3 2   ◇ K 7   ♣ K 2

Three hearts. With shabby texture in both majors and unsupported honor holdings in all suits, this hand should be treated as a minimum. Three notrump would be an error since 14 or 15 HCPs are necessary for this bid.

(4) ♠ A K 3 2   ♡ K J 10 5 2   ◇ —   ♣ 8 6 4 3

Four clubs. Though you are not proud of either the strength of this hand or the quality of your clubs, responder is asking for a description of your shape. Obey the rules and tell him what you have.

(5) ♠ A Q 7 3   ♡ J 10 9 8 6   ◇ A 7   ♣ K 3

Three notrump. Three spades, showing a maximum 4-5-2-2 distribution, would be inaccurate since it would not convey the excellent minor suit holdings.

The two notrump response is appropriate with a wide range of hands. Responder may be exploring the possibility of game based on opener's minor suit distribution or he might be preparing a move towards slam.

Let's look at a few hands showing the two notrump response in action.

(1)

North
- ♠ K J 3 2
- ♡ A K 5 4 2
- ◇ J 6 4
- ♣ 2

South
- ♠ A Q 10 4
- ♡ J 10 7
- ◇ 10 5 3
- ♣ K Q J

North	East	South	West
2 ◇	Pass	2 NT	Pass
3 ◇	Pass	3 ♠	Pass
Pass	Pass		

South, holding opening bid values and a fit in both majors, resisted the temptation to leap directly to game because of his diamond losers. When North's three diamond bid revealed the terrible duplication in clubs, South settled for the part score. If North had shown a singleton diamond, South would have quickly bid a spade game.

(2)

North
♠ A Q 8 5
♡ K J 10 9 7
◇ Q 7 6
♣ 8

South
♠ K J 10 3
♡ Q 4
◇ K 10 2
♣ 5 4 3 2

North	East	South	West
2 ◇	Pass	2 NT	Pass
3 ◇	Pass	4 ♠	Pass
Pass	Pass		

Although a game try with only nine high card points may seem overaggressive, South's optimism was based on his well placed major suit cards plus a proven spade fit. When North rebid three diamonds, South knew that all of his cards were "working" and took a calculated risk by leaping to four spades. A great strength of Flannery is the ability to closely calculate effective versus duplicated values.

(3)

North
- ♠ A 10 5 2
- ♡ A Q 7 6 3
- ◇ J 7 6
- ♣ 2

South
- ♠ K Q 6
- ♡ 4
- ◇ A K Q 9 8 4
- ♣ J 5 4

North	East	South	West
2 ◇	Pass	2 NT	Pass
3 ◇	Pass	4 NT	Pass
5 ♡	Pass	6 ◇	Pass
Pass	Pass		

South bid two notrump, prepared for all eventualities. A three notrump rebid by opener was, of course, impossible, since that would show stoppers in both minors. If opener rebid three clubs, showing a three card club suit, responder intended to try three notrump. If opener rebid three of either major or four clubs, South intended to try four spades as the best chance of success. When North rebid three diamonds, responder's hand grew to giant proportions. Four notrump was correct since the knowledge that opener was dealt a singleton club made aces the only critical factor. When North showed two aces, South contracted for the excellent slam.

(4)

North
- ♠ A K J 7
- ♡ J 5 4 3 2
- ◊ A 9 7
- ♣ 3

South
- ♠ Q 10 6 2
- ♡ 8
- ◊ K Q J 8 2
- ♣ A 7 5

North	East	South	West
2 ◊	Pass	2 NT	Pass
3 ◊	Pass	4 ♣	Pass
4 ◊	Pass	4 ♠	Pass
5 ♠	Pass	6 ♠	Pass
Pass	Pass		

A brilliant and subtle auction; the product of a well practiced partnership. North knew that South's four club call was a cuebid; with a real suit, he could have bid three clubs, which they played as forcing, directly over two diamonds. With this in mind, he cuebid his ace of diamonds.

When South established the trump suit by bidding four spades, North acted again. South had made an overture towards slam before bidding four spades, but was afraid to press on because of the weakness of his trump suit. North's five spade bid was intended to convey that trumps were not a problem, but there was danger in the heart suit. South understood the message; with his singleton heart, he contracted for the small slam.

FLANNERY VARIANTS

There seems to be as many modifications to Flannery as there are practiced partnerships who play the convention. Most of these variants are playable and provide added information in exchange for some degree of flexibility. The following is a brief description of the more popular variants favored by the Flannery connoiseur.

(A) Flannery with a six card heart suit. Assume you are dealt:

♠ A J 5 3　♡ K Q 10 8 5 4　◊ K 3　♣ 4

You open with one heart and partner responds with one notrump. If you've agreed to play Flannery, responder might have passed a four card spade suit and you may miss a 4-4 spade fit. To circumvent this possibility, some partnerships have agreed to expand the convention to allow for 4-6 as well as 4-5 major suit distributions.

If responder bids two notrump, asking for further clarification of opener's distribution and strength, a slight modification is needed to let responder know about the sixth heart.

Three clubs	= 4-5-1-3 distribution
Three diamonds	= 4-5-3-1 distribution
Three hearts	= 4-5-2-2 minimum
Three spades	= 4-5-2-2 maximum
Three notrump	= 4-6-?-? (showing the sixth heart)

Please notice that the descriptive rebids are essentially the same except that three notrump now shows a sixth heart instead of a hand with good minor suit cards.

Some theorists believe that using the three notrump bid to show the sixth heart "gives away" too much. They use three spades instead, keeping the original meaning of three notrump, with three hearts showing 4-5-2-2 distribution without defining the strength of the hand.

Whichever modification is selected, some descriptive feature must be sacrificed in order to show the extra heart. However, the security of not missing a 4-4 spade fit is compensation enough for the small degree of lost descriptive accuracy.

As with any optional treatment, the best way to determine whether this modification suits your style is to try it!

(B) Three clubs nonforcing. This method, favored by Bill Flannery, uses a three club response to show a subminimum hand with long clubs. (With a subminimum hand containing long diamonds, responder will merely pass partner's two diamond opening bid). Thus, looking at:

♠ 8 7　♡ J　◊ 9 7 3 2　♣ K Q 9 7 4 3

responder would bid three clubs over partner's two diamond opening bid.

(C) Three clubs artificial. After a two diamond opening, responder probes for three notrump by bidding three clubs in an effort to ascertain opener's ability to help stop one minor. Treating Jxx or Qx or better as a stopper, opener rebids according to the following schedule:

    (a) Three diamonds   = no minor suit stoppers
    (b) Three hearts   = club stopper, no diamond stopper
    (c) Three spades   = diamond stopper, no club stopper
    (d) Three notrump   = both minors stopped

The following type of hand would be appropriate:

♠ K J 4   ♡ Q 6   ◇ A K J 10 5 4   ♣ Q 5

In response to a two diamond opening bid, three notrump would be reasonable if partner has help in the club suit. A bid of three clubs (artificial) will find this out. If opener rebids three hearts or three notrump, all is well. If opener rebids three diamonds or three of either major, three notrump is likely to be unplayable and responder must look elsewhere for a successful contract.

(D) Three diamonds artificial. After a two diamond opening, responder bids three diamonds inaugurating slam exploration. Opener is forced to rebid three hearts, arriving at the following situation:

North	**South**
2 ◇	**3** ◇
3 ♡	

South now defines the intended trump suit. If he bids three spades, this fixes spades as trumps and asks opener to cue bid aces. If South bids anything but three spades, it is a cue bid and fixes the heart suit as trumps. The following hand is an illustration of this treatment:

North
♠ A J 5 2
♡ Q J 10 9 4
◇ A 4
♣ K 5

South
♠ K Q 10 7 3
♡ 2
◇ K Q 3 2
♣ A Q 6

North	East	South	West
2 ◇	Pass	3 ◇[1]	Pass
3 ♡[2]	Pass	3 ♠[3]	Pass
3 NT[4]	Pass	4 ♣[5]	Pass
4 ◇[6]	Pass	4 ♠[7]	Pass
5 ♣[8]	Pass	5 ◇[9]	Pass
5 ♠[10]	Pass	6 ♠[11]	Pass
Pass	Pass		

[1] Major suit slam probe — opener does not know which suit.
[2] Relay allowing responder to specify the trump suit.
[3] Spades are trump (any other bid would specify hearts).
[4] Cue bidding the ace of spades.
[5] Cue bidding the ace of clubs.
[6] Cue bidding the ace of diamonds.
[7] By not cue bidding, responder denies the ace of hearts.
[8] Cue bidding the king of clubs.
[9] Cue bidding the king of diamonds.
[10] Signing off in the face of two potential heart losers.
[11] Based on the singleton heart.

The main disadvantage of these last two treatments is the inability to respond naturally in the minor suits. While we freely admit that there are hands to which these methods are admirably suited, the machinations necessary to reach a minor suit contract make these methods too costly. They are certainly not recommended to any but near-expert players with a very experienced partnership.

Summary

Flannery is a very useful tool for the experienced bridge player. It allows for very accurate hand description with minimum danger. It is not, however, one of these conventions with which you can sit down opposite a stranger and say, "Let's play Flannery" and then go on to the next area of the convention card. It is a complicated convention and therefore best recommended for an established partnership.

THIRD HAND OPENING BIDS

After two passes, it is often sound tactics to open the bidding with less than minimum values. There are several good reasons for such a strategy.

(a) Directing the opening lead:

♠ 5 4   ♡ J 6 3   ◇ A K J 10 4   ♣ J 9 5

Partner is dealer and passes, as does second hand, and it's your turn. If the opponents buy the contact, the defense will probably be served best if partner leads a diamond. Opening this hand one diamond will get partner off to the right lead. (See minus factors — page 125.)

(b) Interference with the opponents' auction.

♠ Q 10 9 5 2   ♡ K 6 5   ◇ A J 2   ♣ 5 4

Both partner and right hand opponent pass. By opening with one spade, you create a possible problem for your left hand opponent. Assume he holds something like:

♠ A J 4   ♡ A J 8 7 3   ◇ 6   ♣ K J 6 2

This is an easy one heart opening bid, but the one spade opening by third hand causes a problem. Although he has adequate point count for a takeout double or an overcall, each has its flaws. Over a takeout double, his partner may bid diamonds. Now a heart rebid would be a distinct overbid. The drawback with a two heart overcall is that the heart suit is rather weak for introduction at the two level. Although the opponents may well land on their feet, the preemptive quality of a one spade opening creates a problem.

(c) The chance to steal a part score.

North
- ♠ A 8 6
- ♡ Q J 9 3
- ◇ Q J 5 4
- ♣ 7 3

West
- ♠ K 10 4 3 2
- ♡ 5
- ◇ A 9 6
- ♣ A Q 9 8

East
- ♠ Q J 7
- ♡ 10 8 2
- ◇ 10 3 2
- ♣ K J 6 5

South
- ♠ 9 5
- ♡ A K 7 6 4
- ◇ K 8 7
- ♣ 10 4 2

North	East	South	West
Pass	Pass	1 ♡	Dbl
3 ♡	?		

What should East bid? Looking at all four hands, it is simple
enough to see that three spades is an easy contract, but virtually impossible to bid. With only seven high card points, a responsive double by East would be quite aggressive, since West might hold only
four spades. Armchair quarterbacks might object to the takeout
double rather than a one spade overcall, but that's unfair — a double is perfectly acceptable with this holding.

If East and South pass the three heart call, the problem reverts
to West. Clearly, K 10 4 3 2 is not nearly a good enough suit to trot
out at the three level. Furthermore, if West does bid three spades,
East will place him with extra values and raise to an unmakable
game. Three hearts, of course, will produce either nine or ten tricks
for North-South, depending on the defense.

We see that an appropriate third hand opening can be a useful
weapon. The trick is in the use of the word appropriate. The
following are some guidelines for determining whether or not to
open a subminimum hand in third seat.

Plus Factors

(1) A five card or longer suit with good texture for lead direction.

(2) A major suit, preferably spades. If the opponent in fourth seat has a lower ranking suit, he must enter the auction at the two level.

(3) High honors (aces and kings) rather than soft values (queens and jacks).

(4) Favorable vulnerability. The general safety and tactical effects of a third hand opening bid are maximal when not vulnerable against vulnerable opponents. And, from a pessimistic point of view, the penalties are not as costly if partner becomes overly ambitious and the opponents double for penalties.

Minus Factors

(1) Scattered values. It is best to have the majority of your high card points concentrated in two or, at most, three suits. A hand such as:

♠ **A K J 6 5**   ♡ **Q J 4**   ◇ **4 3**   ♣ **8 6 4**   **(11 HCPs)**

is a better third seat opener than

♠ **K J 8 4 3**   ♡ **K 3 2**   ◇ **Q 8 4**   ♣ **Q 3**   **(11 HCPs)**

Queens and jacks are defensively oriented cards; don't tell the opponents where they are by an inappropriate third hand opening.

(2) A long minor suit. Since a subminimum opening bid is likely to result in a competitive auction, if you hold the minors, the opponents will be able to compete to the same level of bidding in either major — a definite minus. At the worst, a third hand opening in a minor suit can result in conceding a part score to opponents who, left to their devices, might well have passed out the hand!

(3) Unfavorable vulnerability. A weak third hand opening, vulnerable against non-vulnerable opponents, is dangerous for two reasons. First and most obvious is the potential penalty. Second, and perhaps not so obvious, is that the opponents will compete more freely if not vulnerable and gain a part score on a hand that might normally have been passed out.

With such a plethora of information, determine whether or not to open the bidding in third seat with each of the following hands:

(1) ♠ 5 3   ♡ K Q J 5 4   ◇ A 8 4 3   ♣ 3 2
(Both vulnerable.)

One heart. This is a classic third hand opening. Although this hand contains only ten high card points, nothing is wasted. You can stand a raise of your suit and a heart lead looks most productive for your side should the opponents buy the hand.

(2) ♠ J 9 4 3 2   ♡ K 9 5   ◇ A 3 2   ♣ K 4
(You are vulnerable.)

Pass. Although a one spade opening is certainly tempting, on balance the potential loss is greater than the potential gain. The unfavorable vulnerability increases the danger of a penalty, especially with such a shabby suit. It is also dangerous to direct a spade lead. Partner, looking at:

♠ K 5   ♡ 6 3   ◇ Q J 9 4   ♣ Q 8 7 6 2

will not take kindly to being talked out of his natural lead of the diamond queen in favor of the disastrous lead of the spade king. In general, any subminimum hand with values in all four suits is suspect as a third hand opening bid.

(3) ♠ A K Q J   ♡ 5 3   ◇ J 10 8 7   ♣ 4 3 2
(Neither vulnerable.)

One spade. Yes, this is a book on five card majors, but the advantages of lead direction far outweigh the disadvantage of not holding a fifth spade. Adding to this the preemptive quality of the spade suit, one spade is a standout choice for a third hand opening bid. Score yourself as both alert and flexible if you have little problem with this concept. (Duplicate players are sometimes puzzled by the "seldom" and "never" boxes for four card major openings on the convention card; this is an excellent hand to illustrate "seldom.")

(4) ♠ K J 6 4 3   ♡ K J 4 3   ◇ Q 6 4   ♣ 4
(The opponents are vulnerable.)

One spade. At favorable vulnerability, possession of both majors provides a good chance that your side might be able to steal this hand. Another plus is that you have excellent defense if the opponents play hearts. In any event, they must bid one level higher to earn the right to declare this hand.

(5) ♠ A Q J 10 3   ♡ 5   ◊ K 4 3   ♣ 8 6 5 4
        (You are vulnerable.)

One spade. Even at unfavorable vulnerability, the chance to direct the opening lead and at the same time preempt the entire one level is too juicy to pass up. With such a fine suit there is not much danger of a serious penalty.

Responding to a Third Hand Opening

The only disadvantage of the third hand subminimum opening is that first hand, looking at a maximum pass, is not sure if opener has full values for his opening bid. Assume that you have:

♠ K 5 4 3   ♡ A 9 6 5   ◊ A J 4   ♣ 3 2

This is a "maybe" opening bid which you have elected to pass in first seat. Left hand opponent also passes and partner opens one spade in third seat. Fourth hand passes; although there is a strong temptation to leap directly to game, partner, in third seat, may have a sub-par hand. A limit raise would be a slight underbid because partner may pass with a light opener that is quite sufficient for game.

Or you may hold a bit less, such as:

♠ K 4 3 2   ♡ A 5 4 3   ◊ K 3 2   ♣ 6 5

with the same auction as above. This hand is certainly adequate for a limit raise, but if opener is subminimum, the three level might be too high.

* * * * * * * *

The next section discusses the Drury convention, which aids the partnership to discover if a third hand opener is subminimum.

THE DRURY CONVENTION

The Drury convention is used in non-competitive situations by a passed hand to determine whether partner's third or fourth hand major suit opening bid was subminimum or based on full values.

After a third (or fourth) seat major suit opening bid, two clubs is an artificial response, asking opener to confirm or deny full values for his opening bid. A rebid by opener of his original major warns responder that the opening bid was based on subminimum values or, at best, a hand that barely qualifies as an opener and that would pass a limit raise. Thus:

North	East	South	West
Pass	Pass	1 ♠	Pass
2 ♣	Pass	2 ♠	

or

North	East	South	West
Pass	Pass	1 ♡	Pass
2 ♣	Pass	2 ♡	

shows no game interest. Any rebid by opener other than his original major confirms full values for his opening bid.*

The following three conditions are necessary if Drury is to be effective:

(a) Responder should hold at least three card trump support.

(b) There must be game interest if opener has full values.

(c) The auction is non-competitive.

---

*Drury, as originally designed, used a two diamond rebid to show subminimum values. Since the use of Drury requires a trump fit, it is logical to show the worst hand by rebidding the major suit. Be sure your partner is playing the same way you are.

Assuming you have adopted Drury as part of your five card major bidding repertoire, what is your correct response on each of the following hands? In each case, partner has opened third hand.

(1) ♠ K 5 4 2   ♡ A 9 5   ◇ K 4 3 2   ♣ 8 7
(Partner opens one spade.)

Two clubs. Since game is certainly possible opposite a full opening bid, your first job is to ascertain the quality of partner's hand. If partner rebids anything other than two spades, you should invite game in spades. If partner rebids two spades, you should pass. Opener will almost assuredly fulfill the part score, but might be in danger in any higher contract. The main purpose of Drury is to keep the partnership from getting too high.

(2) ♠ Q 10 4 3   ♡ A 3   ◇ J 9 2   ♣ K J 10 9
(Partner opens one heart.)

One spade. Drury should only be used with a trump fit. At this point in the auction, a fit is yet to be found. Partner will normally pass one spade with a subminimum and take another bid with a full opener.

(3) ♠ 5 3   ♡ K 9 6 5   ◇ A Q J   ♣ J 5 4 2
(Partner opens one heart, RHO overcalls with one spade.)

Three hearts. When the opponents have bid, Drury is off.

(4) ♠ K 3 2   ♡ A 9 7   ◇ K 10 6 4 3   ♣ 5 3
(Partner opens one diamond.)

Three diamonds. The Drury convention only applies over a major suit opening bid. With this hand, a limit raise in diamonds is the winning call. It is a poor practice to open subminimum hands in a short minor suit; if partner has only three diamonds he certainly has full values. If he is subminimum with diamond length, your three diamond response serves as an effective preempt.

(5) ♠ A 7   ♡ Q 6 5   ◇ J 3   ♣ K J 9 7 6 5
(Partner opens one spade.)

One notrump. Since two clubs would be Drury, the forcing notrump is the best alternative. If partner holds full values, he will treat the notrump as forcing. If he passes, and the opponents enter the auction, you can compete in clubs.

Now let's try the other side of the fence. Examine the following auctions and find your proper rebid after you have opened in third seat and partner has responded.

(1) ♠ A K J 5 4   ♡ 8 7 3   ◇ 8 4 2   ♣ K 6

North	East	South	West
Pass	Pass	1 ♠	Pass
2 ♣	Pass	?	

Two spades. By using Drury, partner is signaling aggressive intentions. Your duty is to tell him as quickly as possible that your opening bid is nothing to write home about. This may be sufficient to convert a potential minus score to a plus score. As an example, if partner holds something like:

♠ Q 8 7 3   ♡ A 9 4 2   ◇ A J 5   ♣ 5 4

three spades (a likely contract if not playing Drury), depends on a very favorable placement of the cards, while two spades is a reasonable bet.

(2) ♠ 7   ♡ K Q 10 9 7   ◇ 5 4   ♣ A Q 10 5 4

North	East	South	West
Pass	Pass	1 ♡	Pass
2 ♣	Pass	?	

Three clubs. Although this hand contains only eleven high card points, the distributional advantages are so pronounced that you should take an aggressive view. Remember, Drury guarantees a trump fit so full value should be given to your singleton and doubleton. Add to that the potential trick taking power of the excellent club suit and it should be obvious that a two heart rebid would be criminally conservative.

(3) ♠ K Q 10 5 4   ♡ Q 9   ◇ A Q 9 6 4   ♣ 3

North	East	South	West
Pass	Pass	1 ♠	Pass
2 ♣	Pass	?	

Two diamonds. This is a healthy opening bid and it is your duty to describe your distribution as completely as possible. You are certainly worth a game try opposite partner's Drury call and if he has the perfect hand, slam is not out of the question. Plan to bid diamonds again at your next turn to call.

(4) ♠ A Q J 6 4 3　♡ 5 2　♢ K Q 4 2　♣ 3

North	East	South	West
Pass	Pass	1 ♠	Pass
2 ♣	Dbl	?	

Four spades. A purely tactical call. North is showing interest in game based on a spade fit. We presume that East's double of two clubs shows a good club suit. Your hand is not the greatest in the world, and the spade length is a clue that your side may have little defense against a club contract. Duty to your partnership requires that you make it as difficult as possible for the opponents to contest the bidding.

(5) ♠ A 4 2　♡ A K 7 5 4　♢ 5 3　♣ J 3 2

North	East	South	West
Pass	Pass	1 ♡	Pass
1 NT	Pass	?	

Pass. The straightforward way to advise partner that game is unlikely is to pass his forcing notrump response. (It ceases to be forcing opposite a subminimum or near minimum third hand opener; partner should show support at once if he has it.)

Evaluation

Drury is an excellent tool that serves to keep the level of a contract low opposite a weak third or fourth hand opening. As with all artificial bids, it carries the disadvantage of allowing the opponents to make a no-risk lead directing double. For example, an auction such as:

North	East	South	West
Pass	Pass	1 ♠	Pass
2 ♣	Dbl	Pass	3 ♣

can certainly make you wish you weren't playing Drury. East was able to indicate club values by doubling the artificial bid and West, armed with club length, "raised" partner's clubs forcing a nasty part score decision for North-South. East might be looking at:

♠ 3 2   ♡ Q 10 7   ♢ 7 5 4 3   ♣ A K J 9

which is impossibly dangerous for an overcall, but perfectly safe for a lead directing double. However, the advantages of Drury as outlined in this section definitely outweigh the drawbacks posed by this rare auction.

MINOR SUIT OPENING BIDS

While there is no law which states that an opening bid of one club or one diamond may not be made on a suit of four or more cards, there is always the possibility that opener started with only three cards in his minor suit.

Throughout this section, the theme will be to assume opener holds a three card minor unless the auction implies added length in that suit.

The recommended rebids and responses are in line with modern theory and should negate any problems involved with opening with a three card suit.

Please read this section carefully. Understanding minor suit bidding techniques is essential to the happiness of any five card major partnership.

Choosing a Minor Suit Opening

The rules for determining when and with which suit to inaugurate a minor suit sequence are natural and logical.

(1) With two minors of unequal length, open the bidding with the longer minor regardless of strength or texture.

♠ A 5 4 2   ♡ K J 9 4   ◇ A Q   ♣ 10 7 5
(Open one club.)

♠ A J 8   ♡ J 5 2   ◇ 10 7 5 3   ♣ A K 10
(Open one diamond.)

(2) With two three card minors, open the bidding in the stronger minor. If approximately equal, open one club.

♠ K 5 4 2   ♡ A 10 7   ◇ A K 6   ♣ 10 8 4
(Open one diamond.)

♠ K 5 4 2   ♡ A 10 7   ◇ A 7 6   ♣ K J 4
(Open one club.)

135

(3) With two four card minors, open the bidding with one diamond.*

♠ **A 5 2**   ♡ **K 7**   ◇ **K J 5 2**   ♣ **K 9 5 2**
(Open one diamond.)

♠ **A 5 2**   ♡ **7 4**   ◇ **Q 9 7 3**   ♣ **A K J 4**
(Open one diamond.*)

*Some partnerships agree to open one club with 4-4 minor suit holdings in situations where the clubs are dramatically stronger than diamonds. This is a matter of partnership style and does not materially affect subsequent auctions.

Choose your opening bid on each of the following hands.

(1) ♠ **A K 4**   ♡ **A 8 7 6**   ◇ **A 10 9**   ♣ **A 5 4**

One club. With two three card minors of approximately equal strength, one club provides maximum flexibility.

(2) ♠ **K J 9 8**   ♡ **K J 4**   ◇ **A J 3**   ♣ **K J 7**

One notrump. Three card minors are a convenience, not a necessity. Hope you didn't fall for this one!

(3) ♠ **J 5 4 3 2**   ♡ **A 3**   ◇ **A K J 5 2**   ♣ **2**

One spade. Despite the disparity in strength between the diamonds and spades, it is correct to open with a five card major. If you bid one diamond and partner responds two clubs, a two spade rebid would be a reverse, grossly overstating the strength of the hand.

(4) ♠ **J 5 4 3 2**   ♡ **3**   ◇ **K 4**   ♣ **A K J 9 7**

One club. This holding is the only exception to the rule stated in (3). With five clubs and five spades you bid and rebid spades at your second and third turns to call, thus describing the hand without getting into trouble.

(5) ♠ **A K 5 2**   ♡ **K 5 3 2**   ◇ **A 2**   ♣ **10 5 4**

One club. This type of hand causes the most anxiety to players not used to a five card major structure. Visualizing how the auction might develop should prove that there are no potential problems. If partner responds in either major, you intend to raise. If partner bids one diamond, a one heart rebid is easy. Finally, if partner raises clubs, he is aware that you may hold only three. (We will explore this last concept as we consider responses to minor suit openings.)

Responding to One Club or One Diamond

The development of minor suit auctions is an exercise in determining in which suit to play and how high to play the contract. The following are general guidelines for the initial response.

(a) Bid the longest suit at the one level.

Opener bids one club or one diamond and you hold:

♠ A K 5 2   ♡ J 5 4 3 2   ◇ 9 7 2   ♣ 4
(Respond one heart.)

(b) With two five card suits, bid the higher ranking suit.

Opener bids one club or one diamond and you hold:

♠ 10 9 7 5 4   ♡ A K J 5 4   ◇ 3   ♣ J 7
(Respond one spade.)

(c) With two or more four card suits, bid the lower ranking suit.

Opener bids one club or one diamond and you hold:

♠ A 10 5 4   ♡ A 10 5 4   ◇ 7 5   ♣ Q 7 6
(Respond one heart.)

Opener bids one club and you hold:

♠ A 10 5 4   ♡ A 10 5 4   ◇ Q 7 6 5   ♣ 6
(Respond one diamond.)

(d) With no four card (or longer) major (or four diamonds after a one club opener) and seven to ten high card points, bid one notrump.

Opener bids one club or one diamond and you hold:

♠ A 5 4   ♡ K 7 6   ◇ J 10 3   ♣ Q 5 4 2
(Respond one notrump.)

(e) With five or more cards in partner's minor suit opening, six to ten high card points and no four card major, raise partner's minor to the two level.

Opener bids one club and you hold:

♠ A 3   ♡ 5 4 2   ◇ J 3 2   ♣ K 9 7 4 3
(Raise to two clubs.)

or opener bids one diamond and you hold:

♠ A 3   ♡ 5 4 3   ◇ K 9 7 4 3   ♣ J 3 2

(Raise to two diamonds.)

(f) With five or more cards in partner's minor, no four card (or longer) major and ten to twelve evaluated points, bid three of partner's minor suit. As with jump raises in the majors, this is a limit raise, nonforcing but highly invitational.

Opener bids one club and you hold:

♠ A 5 4   ♡ J 2   ◇ Q 5 4   ♣ K J 10 9 7

(Jump to three clubs.)

Assume partner opens the bidding with one club. What is the correct response with each of the following five hands?

(1) ♠ K 8 5 3   ♡ A 9 8 7   ◇ —   ♣ K 10 8 7 2

One heart. There is a strong temptation to raise opener's clubs with a five card holding, but this runs the risk of missing a 4-4 major suit fit. It is important to remember that opener cannot open a four card major, so all possibilities of a 4-4 major suit fit must be explored as soon as possible.

(2) ♠ A K J 5   ♡ 10 9 8 7   ◇ 6 5   ♣ 8 6 3

One heart. Here again temptation must be resisted. With eight high card points in spades and zero high card points in hearts, there is an urge to respond one spade but this, again, could easily result in missing a 4-4 heart fit. Suppose partner holds:

♠ 7 4   ♡ A K Q 6   ◇ K 7 4   ♣ K 9 7 5

He would rebid one notrump over one spade and you are hardly strong enough to introduce your shabby four card heart suit at that point.

(3) ♠ 6 5 4 3 2   ♡ K Q J 6   ◇ K 5 4   ♣ 6

One spade. Always bid your longest suit first, regardless of high card placement. At this point in the auction you are looking for an eight card trump fit; after partner rebids, you may introduce your hearts. Partner will know that you have five spades and at least four hearts; with two four card suits, you would have bid one heart at your first turn to call.

(4) ♠ Q 9 6 4 3   ♡ A K Q 7 3   ◇ 3   ♣ 4 3

One spade. With two five card suits, bid the higher suit first regardless of the comparative high card content of the suits. If opener fails to support spades, bid the hearts, showing five spades and at least four hearts. A possible auction might be:

Opener	Responder
1 ♣	1 ♠
2 ♣	2 ♡
2 NT	3 ♡

Since you would not rebid hearts without at least five cards in the suit, opener will now know that you hold five hearts; since you bid spades first, he will also know that you hold at least five spades.

(5) ♠ Q 10 9 ♡ Q 10 9 ◇ Q 10 8 ♣ K 5 4 3

One notrump. This bid denies four diamonds, four hearts or four spades, so you are implying at least four card club support. (A no-trump response to a one diamond opener implies either length in clubs or diamonds.)

Exploratory Rebids

As mentioned so many times, the object of most bidding sequences is to locate either an eight card or better fit in a suit or to land in some number of notrump. Only after locating the fit do we determine how high the contract should be. While this is by no means a 100% rule, considering most bidding sequences in this manner provides a good insight into the mechanics of auctioneering. It is critical to a successful exploration process that both partners show four card holdings as long as partner might have a fit.

Examine the following sequence of bidding:

South	West	North	East
1 ♣	Pass	1 ◇	Pass
1 ♡	Pass	1 ♠	Pass
1 NT	Pass	?	

Let's translate the "code" into English.

(South: One club.) I have at least three clubs and no five card major (unless I hold five clubs and five spades). I have anywhere from twelve points up to twenty-odd.

(North: One diamond.) I hold a hand of undetermined strength (probably less than 17 points), four or more diamonds and probably no five card major (with 5-5 I would have bid the major).

(South: One heart.) You still don't know how many points I have, though it's probably under nineteen since I did not jump shift. However, I do hold four hearts.

(North: One spade.) We do not have a 4-4 heart fit; I do, however, have four spades. Does that turn you on?

(South: One notrump.) No. We don't have an eight card major fit. In addition, my maximum holding is fifteen high card points. If I had more, I'd have bid differently.

This process of bidding up the line is often referred to as "one-over-one" and conveys a great deal of pertinent information. Please notice that during this hypothetical auction, North has not really shown the exact strength of his hand, although both his bids were forcing. He might hold:

♠ K 9 7 5   ♡ 3 2   ◇ A 5 4 3 2   ♣ J 9

in which case he will pass one notrump. Or he might hold:

♠ A Q 7 6   ♡ J 4   ◇ A Q 7 6   ♣ J 3 2

in which case he will leap to three notrump. Either of these hands would be consistent with the auction.

Another nice feature of one-over-one bidding is the exclusion concept. To illustrate, you hold:

♠ Q J 3   ♡ Q 10 9 8   ◇ K 5 4 3   ♣ Q 7

Partner opens one club, you respond one diamond and partner rebids one spade. You need not worry about missing an eight card heart fit; partner's failure to rebid one heart excluded the possibility of his holding four hearts. You can therefore rebid one notrump in complete confidence. If partner raises, game should be attempted. If he passes, one notrump should not present many difficulties.

Notice that with a stronger hand:

♠ A J 3   ♡ K 10 9 8   ◇ K J 5 4   ♣ Q 6

assuming the same bidding sequence, you can jump in notrump without disclosing your excellent heart holding to the opposition.

As should be evident, a great deal of information can be gleaned from proper interpretation of the bidding. The following hands illustrate some common inferential sequences.

You have opened the bidding with one club on each of the following hands. Examine the auction and make the appropriate rebid based on the evolution of the auction.

(1) ♠ A 4   ♡ A K J 2   ◊ 5 4 3   ♣ Q 6 5 4

You	Partner
1 ♣	1 ♠
?	

One notrump. If responder holds a reasonable hand with five spades and four or more hearts, he will normally bid two hearts (nonforcing) over the one notrump rebid. Your hand is too weak to bid hearts at this point.

(2) ♠ K 5 4 3   ♡ A 6 4 2   ◊ 9 6   ♣ A Q 2

You	Partner
1 ♣	1 ♡
?	

Two hearts. Show your fit at the earliest opportunity. One spade would not be forcing; partner, with a minimum and no fit, might pass, leaving you in an unpleasant contract. Responder will never believe that opener has four-card support for hearts unless opener supports immediately.

(3) ♠ K J 5 4   ♡ A Q 9 6   ◊ K   ♣ A J 5 2

You	Partner
1 ♣	1 ◊
1 ♡	1 ♠
?	

Three spades. The first two bids for each side explored for a spot to play. Despite a robust 18 high card points, opener was content with a simple rebid of one heart; his singleton king of diamonds is not appetizing. Having located a fit in spades, opener jumps to the three level, inviting partner to bid a game with any reasonable hand.

(4) ♠ K 4 3   ♡ J 3   ◊ A 2   ♣ A Q 7 5 4 2

You	Partner
1 ♣	1 ♠
2 ♣	2 ♡
?	

Three spades. The auction has greatly enhanced the value of this hand. Under the rules of "one-over-one" responder's rebid of two hearts guarantees a five card spade suit. With this in mind, opener's two red suit doubletons are likely to be very useful. In addition, his strong six card club suit should prove to be a source of tricks. By bidding three spades, opener is saying," I have a minimum, but this minimum will be a very welcome dummy for you."

(5) ♠ 6 3 2   ♡ K J 7   ◊ K J 9   ♣ K Q J 8

You	Partner
1 ♣	1 ♠
1 NT	2 ◊
?	

Two spades. Compare this hand with example (4). Although you have a proven eight card spade fit (if partner had four spades and four diamonds, he would have responded one diamond to your opening bid), game is unlikely unless responder can make another move. This hand contains no ruffing values, no aces, and no long suit. However, if responder tries for game in the light of the discouraging rebid, opener should accept, based on his good high cards in responder's diamond suit.

Let us examine the evolution of some auctions which illustrate the "Where-How High" principle.

North
- ♠ K Q 8 5 3
- ♡ K 4 3
- ◇ A 7 2
- ♣ A 9

South
- ♠ A 7 6 2
- ♡ A 8
- ◇ K J 4 3
- ♣ J 8 6

South	North
1 ◇	1 ♠
2 ♠	3 ♣
3 ♠	4 ◇
4 ♡	6 ♠

South's rebid of two spades settled the "Where?" question. The second problem is "How high?" North's three club rebid is somewhat ambiguous. It could be a try for game, needing help in clubs or a cue bid as a prelude to a slam-going sequence.

Since his clubs would not be of much help, South merely rebid the four card spade suit.

North now clarified his slammish intention by cue bidding his ace of diamonds. When South responded by cue bidding the ace of hearts, this was all North needed to bid the small slam in spades.

North
♠ 5
♡ A Q 8 6 5 3
♢ 2
♣ A K 9 7 2

South
♠ Q J 10 4
♡ K 7 4 2
♢ A Q 6 5
♣ 3

South	North
1 ♢	1 ♡
2 ♡	4 NT
5 ♢	6 ♡

South's two heart raise again clarified "Where?" There was no need to muddy the waters by introducing his four card spade suit. When a trump fit has been found, support partner as quickly as possible so you can concentrate on "How high?" North now bid four notrump and was somewhat disappointed to find partner with only one ace. He settled for the small slam. Notice that while there are all sorts of slam conventions available, clear cut situations should not be clouded — North is mostly concerned about aces and Blackwood is the easiest route.

North
- ♠ A Q 6 5 3
- ♡ J 8 6 4
- ◊ K 3
- ♣ 9 5

South
- ♠ K 8 7 2
- ♡ Q 5 3
- ◊ A 7 5 4
- ♣ K J

South	North
1 ◊	1 ♠
2 ♠	3 ♡
3 ♠	Pass

As in a previous example, North's three heart bid is either a game try or the beginning of a move towards slam. Opener is asked to make a decision; with absolutely nothing extra, coupled with minimum help in the heart suit, he made a discouraging rebid of three spades. Although North certainly had his game try, with ten high card points and two doubletons, he has nothing more and settles for a part score. (On a good day, this hand might make game, but even three spades could be too high.)

Raising Partner's Minor

We mentioned direct raises earlier, but some elaboration may prove helpful. Sometimes it is correct for responder to raise opener's minor at his first turn to call. Except for suit length, the requirements for such raises are similar to the requirements for a raise of a major suit opening bid.

(a) A simple raise (from the one level to the two level) is non invitational, showing six to nine points.

(b) A jump to the three level (one club-three clubs or one diamond-three diamonds) shows limit raise values and is game invitational.

There are two distributional rules:

(1) Responder must not hold a four card major suit.

(2) Responder should hold at least five card support.

The reason behind not holding a four card major is obvious. Assume you hold:

♠ **J 4 3 2**　♡ **9**　◊ **K 8 6 5 3**　♣ **A 9 7**

and partner starts the auction with one diamond. There is a strong temptation to raise partner's diamonds and ignore the shabby spade suit. Yet this could lead to a bidding disaster. Opener might hold:

♠ **A Q 9 8**　♡ **8 6 5 4**　◊ **A Q 4**　♣ **6 5**

and a spade game has excellent chance for success. Opener is not nearly strong enough to introduce his spade suit over a simple two diamond response. Please notice that if the auction goes:

Opener	Responder
1 ◊	1 ♠
2 ♠	

it is more than reasonable for responder to try for game. In addition to eight high card points, he has valuable added assets in the singleton heart and the diamond fit.

The reason for not raising partner's minor without five card support is just as straightforward — opener might have started with only a three card suit. With only four card support for a minor opening and no four card major, a notrump response is normally correct.

The following hands serve to illustrate the handling of minor suit actions.

(1) ♠ **Q 3**　♡ **J 5 4 3**　◊ **A 9 6 5 4 2**　♣ **J**
　　　(Partner opens one diamond.)

One heart. Resist raising partner's diamonds and stay disciplined by showing the four card heart suit. We cannot overemphasize the importance of this principle. When employing a five card major structure, a major suit response is the **only** correct answer; bypassing a major suit to raise partner's minor is simply wrong.

(2) ♠ J 9 5   ♡ 3   ◇ K 10 6 3   ♣ A Q 8 5 2
   (Partner opens one club.)

Three clubs. With ten high card points, no four card major and good five card club support, this hand is worth a limit raise. At this juncture, we would like to make an interesting point. A limit raise in a major suit is invitational to a major suit game; opener either passes or bids four (or more) of the indicated major. A limit raise in a minor suit is still invitational, but it often encourages opening bidder to bid game in notrump. The reasons for this are:

(a) Most of the time, a 4-4 trump fit will gain a trick over playing in notrump, so three notrump and four of a major stand equal chances of success. However, the difference between a minor suit game and a notrump game is **two** tricks.

(b) For duplicate players, collecting ten tricks in notrump produces a higher score than eleven tricks in a minor. This matchpoint advantage is sufficient to sway the duplicate player to take his chances on a notrump game.

(3) ♠ 7 5   ♡ A 9 6   ◇ K Q 2   ♣ K Q 9 5 3
   (Partner opens one club.)

One diamond! This hand (and other distributions like it) is extremely awkward to bid. With fourteen high card points, you are certainly pleased to hear partner open the bidding. However, examine your choices. Your hand is far too strong for either a simple raise or a jump to three clubs, since neither of these bids are forcing. A jump to two notrump is ill-conceived considering the utter lack of a spade stopper. The diamond response is a temporizing bid to allow partner to describe his opening values.

(4) ♠ A K J 3   ♡ 7 5 3 2   ◇ 9 6 5   ♣ A 8
   (Partner opens one diamond.)

One heart. Just a reminder! Once again, with two four card major suits, bid the lower suit regardless of the texture. Game is very likely opposite your twelve high card points, but your first task is to look for a 4-4 major suit fit. The danger of responding one spade instead of one heart should be obvious. Opener might hold:

♠ 8 7   ♡ A K 10 5   ◇ A K 7 4 3   ♣ 9 7

in which case, after the auction one diamond—one spade, it becomes awkward to find the heart fit. Opener is too weak to introduce the heart suit at the two level, and a rebid of two hearts by responder would promise five spades.

147

(5) ♠ A 9 5 ♡ 3 ◊ A 6 5 ♣ K Q 7 5 4 3
(Partner opens one club.)

Once again, one diamond. This hand is far too strong for an invitational auction and leaping to three notrump would be nonsensical
with a singleton heart. For the imaginative reader who took our
statement about the similarity between major and minor suit raises
literally, a three heart splinter bid stands out. Yes, splinter bids are
available as part of minor suit auctions. As with major suit
splinters, this bid shows opening bid values in support of opener's
suit plus a singleton or void in the splinter suit. Notice also that the
splinter takes into consideration the possibility that partner may
hold only a three card minor suit, so it guarantees at least five card
trump support.

In the context of our bidding structure, both the standard two
notrump response, showing 13-15 high card points, and the three
notrump response, showing 16-18 high card points, are really
wasted. Minor suit auctions are best served by having the two notrump response describe a balanced hand of eleven to twelve high
card points, stoppers in the three other suits and no four card major. The three notrump response should show the same type of
hand with 13 to 15 high card points. (If you are fortunate enough to
pick up a balanced hand with 16 or 17 high card points, you will
certainly be creative enough to find ways to keep the auction open
and to explore for slam.)

To recapitulate:

> 1 of a minor — 2 NT = 11-12 HCP
> 1 of a minor — 3 NT = 13-15 HCP

Let's look at a few examples.

(1) ♠ A J 3 ♡ A 6 5 ◊ Q 10 6 ♣ 10 8 7 6
(Partner opens one club or one diamond.)

Two notrump. You have an eleven point balanced hand with stoppers in the three unbid suits and no four card major. Let your partner know this good news immediately by bidding two notrump. He
can now determine the course of the auction. Since the two notrump response to one of a minor is a limit bid, opener can (and
should) pass with a balanced minimum.

(2) ♠ 8 7   ♡ K 8 7 4   ◇ A Q J 10 9   ♣ 7 6
      (Partner opens one diamond.)

One heart. Always show the four card major suit first.

(3) ♠ K J 10   ♡ Q J 9   ◇ A J 9   ♣ Q 7 5 4
      (Partner opens one club or one diamond.)

Three notrump. After either minor suit opening, describe this hand completely by bidding game in notrump. Please remember that this is **not** a shut out bid. If partner has unusual distribution or extra values, he can bid again.

At this point you should have a comprehensive understanding of minor suit opening bids and be prepared to go into battle armed with the knowledge that starting the bidding with a three card minor suit is no bogeyman to scare you away from the system.

* * *

The next section contains two conventional treatments associated with minor suit openings. These are inverted minors and new minor forcing. Unlike the two major suit conventions (the negative double and the forcing notrump), these are not necessary to the success or failure of your methods. However, they do come highly recommended and will definitely increase the accuracy of your auctions.

Optional Conventions

INVERTED MINOR SUIT RAISES

Since strength showing minor suit support bids tend to invite three notrump (unlike strength showing major support which aims towards four of the major), situations can occur where opener cannot make an intelligent decision. As an example, assume opener holds:

♠ A 7 5 2   ♡ 7 4   ◇ A 5   ♣ A Q 8 6 4

In response to his one club opening bid, responder bids three clubs (limit raise). What to do? Three notrump might be very dangerous because possibly neither opener or responder may have a heart stopper. Let's assume opener bids three spades, hoping partner will bid three notrump with a heart stopper. Responder may hold:

♠ Q 6   ♡ K Q 10   ◇ J 10 8   ♣ K 9 7 3 2

in which case three notrump is a fine contract. But he may hold:

♠ K Q   ♡ A 2   ◇ 9 3 2   ♣ J 10 9 7 5 3

Now both three notrump and a slam in clubs depend on the location of the club king. Five clubs is, of course, quite cold, but responder doesn't know about the diamond control.

To solve this problem and leave room for investigation, theorists have **inverted** the meaning of minor suit raises. Playing "inverted minors," a jump raise shows less than eight points and is primarily preemptive, while a simple raise shows **at least** limit raise values and is forcing, though not necessarily to game.

The Preemptive Minor Suit Jump Raise

After an opening bid of one club or one diamond, a jump by responder to three of partner's suit (assuming that the opponents have not bid or doubled):

(a) Shows at least five card trump support.

(b) Denies a four card major.

(c) Shows less than eight points.

(d) Is primarily intended as preemptive.

To illustrate, partner opens one diamond and you are dealt the following depressing array:

♠ K 3   ♡ 5 3 2   ◇ Q J 7 6 5 4   ♣ 3 2

A jump to three diamonds would be a good preemptive action **whether or not RHO bids.** If partner holds a useful hand, all well and good. But partner may hold a normal hand such as:

♠ 5 4 2   ♡ A 5 4   ◇ A K 10 9 8   ♣ K 8

In this case the opponents are almost sure to make a spade game and maybe even a slam! By jumping to three diamonds you describe the potential uselessness of your hand for defensive purposes. Please notice that an astute opening bidder will continue the preemption by bidding five diamonds, forcing a nasty decision on the opponents.

Since the type of hand suited for a jump to three of partner's minor ranges from under average to awful, the opening bidder often has a problem on how to react to this information.

Consider the following bidding situations. In each case, you (North) have opened the bidding. In addition, your opponents have decided not to be preempted easily, so a couple of the following sequences will put you to a real test.

(1) ♠ A 5 4 3   ♡ K J 9 8   ◇ A J 2   ♣ J 7

North	East	South	West
1 ◇	Dbl	3 ◇	4 ◇
?			

Pass. Don't let West's cue bid frighten you. Your short diamond holding makes it likely that your side will score at least one diamond trick. In addition, your length and strength in the majors should provide plenty of deterrence to any East-West game. Stay passive, planning to defend by leading diamonds at every opportunity in an effort to cut down the opposing trump length. Partner should not bid again after having made a preemptive call.

(2) ♠ 3   ♡ A J 9 8   ◊ A 10 8 7 6 5   ♣ A 5

North	East	South	West
1 ◊	Dbl	3 ◊	3 ♡
5 ◊	5 ♡	Pass	Pass
?			

Six diamonds. Resist the temptation to take an almost sure profit by doubling five hearts. The potential of this hand is so great that a bit of greed is in order. Given that partner has at most one heart and at least five diamonds, there is a strong chance that a small slam in diamonds might be dependent on the lead or just plain cold. For example, a possible South hand might be:

♠ K 7 6   ♡ 3   ◊ K 9 4 3 2   ♣ J 9 8 7

Unless the opponents lead a club, the king of spades will provide a parking place for the losing club, presuming the ace is "on side." (If the spade king were the club king, the lead wouldn't matter.)

(3) ♠ Q J 10 9   ♡ K Q 10 7   ◊ J 2   ♣ A 10 9

North	East	South	West
1 ♣	Dbl	3 ♣	4 ♠
?			

Double. Your opening bid, though minimum, is going to produce a lot of tricks. Partner's preempt has done a good job of precipitating the opponents to undertake what promises to be a nightmarish contract against only a part score for your side.

(4) ♠ K 10 3   ♡ K Q 4   ◊ A K 3 2   ♣ A 4 3

North	East	South	West
1 ◊	Pass	3 ◊	Dbl
?			

Three notrump. With 19 high card points, this bid is hard to resist. South, although weak, promises at least five diamonds; a key jack or two may be enough for nine tricks.

(5) ♠ A 9 7 6   ♡ 6   ◇ K Q J 10 8   ♣ K 7 6

North	East	South	West
1 ◇	Pass	3 ◇	Pass
?			

Five diamonds, continuing the preempt. The opponents failed to bid the first time around. Don't give them a second chance. Your side has virtually no defense and any opportunity to compound the preempt should not be overlooked. Of course, as with any purely sacrificial bid, vulnerability is the deciding factor. If vulnerable against non vulnerable opponents, a pass would be the discrete action. Otherwise, stand or fall with five diamonds.

The Strong Single Minor Suit Raise

After an opening bid of one club or one diamond, a raise to two of partner's suit (assuming that the opponents have not bid or doubled):

(a) Shows at least four trumps.*

(b) Denies a four card major.

(c) Promises at least nine points.

(d) Has an unlimited upper range.

(e) Is forcing for one round.

Assume partner opens one club. Which of these five hands would not qualify for a raise to two clubs?

(1) ♠ A 5 4   ♡ K 7 3   ◇ 3 2   ♣ A K Q J 10

(2) ♠ A 2   ♡ 4 3 2   ◇ K 9 5 4 3   ♣ A Q J

(3) ♠ A K 3   ♡ 3 2   ◇ 10 7 5   ♣ K J 9 7 3

(4) ♠ 5 3   ♡ A 7 6 3   ◇ 9 3 2   ♣ A Q J 10

(5) ♠ K 4   ♡ Q 7   ◇ A 5 3   ♣ Q 10 9 8 7 6

Pretty easy, right? Hands (2) and (4) are inappropriate. Hand (2) contains only three trumps, while hand (4) contains a four card major.

*Four trumps are acceptable because the partnership can stop in two notrump.

Rebids After The Inverted Minor Single Raise

The main advantage of inverted raises is the extra room available for exploration. Since the single raise can be anything from nine points to a slam try, opener is obliged to bid again. There are many different rebid styles; everybody and his brother has their own method. However, the following schedule of rebids is workable, easy to learn, logical, and should provide responder with sufficient information to make an intelligent rebid decision.

The bidding has gone:
1 of a minor — 2 of a minor (inverted)

Rebid	Strength	Status	Characteristics
2 NT	Minimum (12-13)	Nonforcing	Stoppers in both majors
3 NT	Extra Values	Nonforcing	Stoppers in both majors
2 ♡	Undetermined	Forcing	Heart stopper; probably no spade stopper
2 ♠	Undetermined	Forcing	Spade stopper; probably no heart stopper
3 ♡, 3 ♠	Undetermined	Forcing	Highly distributional

The bidding has gone:
1 club — 2 clubs (inverted)

3 ♣	Minimum	Nonforcing	4 + clubs, weak majors
2 ♢	Undetermined	Forcing	Minor two suiter (5-4 +)

The bidding has gone:
1 diamond — 2 diamonds (inverted)

3 ♣	Undetermined	Forcing	Minor two suiter (5-4 +)
3 ♢	Minimum	Nonforcing	4 + diamonds, weak majors

Now examine the following five hands. In each case, you've opened the bidding one diamond and partner responded two diamonds. Consult the schedule of responses and determine the correct rebid.

	You	**Partner**
	1 ◊	2 ◊

(1) ♠ K 10 7   ♡ A Q 4 2   ◊ K J 5   ♣ J 10 8

Three notrump. With both major suits stopped the choice is between two notrump and three notrump. Keeping in mind that responder promised at least limit raise values and that he is likely to have at least five diamonds, a nonforcing two notrump would be conservative. Even if dummy is as weak as:

♠ J 2   ♡ K 5 3   ◊ A 10 9 7 6   ♣ Q 7 4

three notrump depends only on locating the queen of diamonds.

(2) ♠ A Q 5 4 3   ♡ 3   ◊ A Q 5 4 3 2   ♣ 7

Three spades. As indicated on the chart, this bid shows a five card spade suit with longer diamonds. Despite the minimum high card range, the distribution plus the proven diamond fit makes this an excellent playing hand. (With five spades and five diamonds, one spade would have been the correct opening bid.)

(3) ♠ A K J   ♡ 3 2   ◊ A Q J 5 4   ♣ A 7 4

Two spades. With 19 high card points opposite a partner who has positive values, prospects are rosy, but the weakness in hearts precludes an immediate notrump call. By bidding two spades, partner will know about your concern with the heart suit. You can describe the good news about the quality of your hand later in the auction.

(4) ♠ J 7   ♡ 5 4 2   ◊ A Q 10 9 8   ♣ A J 7

Three diamonds. Despite the probable ten card diamond fit, game is unlikely unless partner holds extra values. By raising to three diamonds, you've warned partner that he must cover a lot of holes to make game a real possibility. With this weak opening, all you can do is honor the forcing quality of his inverted raise.

(5) ♠ 5 4   ♡ A 7   ◊ K Q 10 5 4   ♣ A J 10 9

Three clubs. Here you must decide whether to show the heart stopper or describe the shape of the hand. In general, it is better to describe your distribution.

After opener's rebid, responder may do one of three things;

(a) Pass a nonforcing bid with minimum values.

(b) Continue the exploratory process.

(c) Bid a game.

Note: A bid of two notrump or three of the original minor **by either opener or responder** is nonforcing. Thus, on the following auctions:

(a) **North South**
   1 ◇   2 ◇
   2 NT 3 ◇

(b) **North South**
   1 ♣   2 ♣
   2 ◇   2 NT

(c) **North South**
   1 ◇   2 ◇
   2 ♠   2 NT
   3 ◇

all of the last bids are nonforcing.

Let's look at the complete auction on each of these hands:

(1)

North
♠ A Q J
♡ 7 6 3
◇ A Q 10 9 8
♣ K 7

South
♠ K 10 7
♡ A Q 4 2
◇ K J 5
♣ J 10 8

South	North
1 ◇	2 ◇
3 NT	4 NT
Pass	

South's three notrump rebid was based on healthy values plus good spot cards. With sixteen high card points, North raised to four notrump; South was expected to pass with a minimum and press on with a maximum. Since he had minimum values for his three notrump rebid, South passed.

(2)

North
- ♠ K J 7
- ♡ Q 8 6
- ◊ K 9 8 7 6
- ♣ A 4

South
- ♠ A Q 5 4 3
- ♡ 3
- ◊ A Q 5 4 3 2
- ♣ 7

South	North
1 ◊	2 ◊
3 ♠	4 ♣
4 ◊	4 ♠
6 ◊	Pass

North's four club rebid is a fully justified cue bid. His excellent spade holding definitely improved his hand. South continued by showing first round control of diamonds. North's four spade bid pinpointed an honor in spades and warned South that the ace of hearts was missing. This was sufficient for South to leap with confidence to the small slam. Notice that six spades would be a much more dangerous contract, since there is a real chance that East-West might negotiate a diamond ruff.

(3)

North
♠ 3 2
♡ J 5 4
♦ K 9 7 6 2
♣ K Q J

South
♠ A K J
♡ 3 2
♦ A Q J 5 4
♣ A 7 4

South	North
1 ♦	2 ♦
2 ♠	3 ♦
4 ♣	4 ♦
5 ♦	Pass

North's three diamond rebid is nonforcing, showing minimum values and no heart stopper. (With a heart stopper, he might have bid two notrump.) South is still looking for slam and shows a strong hand by cue bidding his ace of clubs. North continues his lukewarm attitude by rebidding four diamonds. South gives up on slam and bids game. The defense cashes two hearts and South claims the balance.

(4)

North
- ♠ 8 4
- ♡ A K 4
- ◇ K 7 5 3 2
- ♣ K 5 4

South
- ♠ J 7
- ♡ 5 4 2
- ◇ A Q 10 9 8
- ♣ A J 7

South	North
1 ◇	2 ◇
3 ◇	4 ◇
Pass	

Even though South showed subminimum values, North felt that with a full opening hand he was entitled to one more game try. South had nothing to spare and passed the final invitation. With the club finesse working, South was able to scamper home with ten tricks. Please notice that three notrump, after a spade lead, goes set at least one trick.

(5)

North
- ♠ A 3
- ♡ 5 4 2
- ◊ A 9 7 6 3
- ♣ K Q 7

South
- ♠ 5 4
- ♡ A 7
- ◊ K Q 10 5 4
- ♣ A J 10 9

South	North
1 ◊	2 ◊
3 ♣	3 ♠
3 NT	4 ♣
4 ♡	6 ◊
Pass	

A subtle auction. In the light of South's three club rebid, North's hand improved enormously. All of his cards were "working," especially the king-queen of clubs. His three spade rebid was ambiguous. It might be the prelude to a slam try or simply looking for a heart stopper for notrump. After South bid three notrump, North clarified the situation by rebidding four clubs. South cue bid his ace of hearts which was all North needed to hear to proceed directly to a small slam.

South won the opening spade lead. After drawing trumps, he pitched dummy's spade loser on his fourth club and conceded a heart.

Summary

Inverted minors are a useful adjunct to any partnership methods. The combined ability to preempt the opponents with weak hands and keep the auction low with strong hands makes this a very potent tool. Traditionalists argue that the very accuracy of inverted minors draws a road map for the defense. That occasional occurrence is more than offset by the ability to stay out of bad contracts and to bid good ones. After all, that's what conventions are all about.

NEW MINOR FORCING

The new minor forcing convention is a way for responder to show game interest after a sequence of one of a minor — one of a major — one notrump. Responder would now bid the other minor if he wishes to ask opener for more information about his hand.

Assume opener bids one diamond, responder bids one spade and opener rebids one notrump. With:

♠ A Q 7 6 5   ♡ K J 5 3   ◇ 3 2   ♣ J 2

responder should bid two hearts, planning to accept any invitation opener might issue. But suppose responder holds:

♠ K 9 7 6 4   ♡ K J 5 3   ◇ 3   ♣ 5 4 2

he would make the same two heart bid, but he would also be reciting a quiet prayer for opener to pass.

The new minor forcing response to a one notrump rebid by opener is designed to differentiate between these two types of hands and to explore for a major suit fit.

After the sequence:

South	North
1 ◇	1 ♠
1 NT	

two clubs by North would be artificial, forcing for one round and game invitational. Similarly, had South opened with one club and rebid one notrump over partner's major, two diamonds would be the forcing bid. "New minor forcing" asks opener to clarify his distribution either by showing a three card fit in responder's major suit or by introducing a four card holding in the other major.

163

Opener	Responder	(or)	Opener	Responder
1 ◇	1 ♡ (♠)		1 ♣	1 ♡(♠)
1 NT	2 ♣*		1 NT	2 ◇*

*New minor forcing.

Now consider the original bidding problem. After the auction:

Opener	Responder
1 ◇	1 ♠
1 NT	

if responder holds:

♠ A Q 7 6 5   ♡ K J 5 3   ◇ 3 2   ♣ J 5

he would rebid two clubs (artificial), showing an interest in game and asking opener to further clarify his hand. Holding:

♠ K 9 7 6 4   ♡ K J 5 3   ◇ 3   ♣ 5 4 2

responder would rebid two hearts showing five spades and at least four hearts **with no interest in game.**

To employ new minor forcing, responder should have:

(a) At least nine high card points.
(b) A five card major **or**
(c) Five spades and at least four hearts.

The auction has gone:

North	South
1 ♣	1 ♠
1 NT	?

What should South bid on the following hands?

(1) ♠ A K 7 6 4   ♡ K 10 9 7   ◇ 4   ♣ K 7 6

Two diamonds. Since two hearts would not be forward-going, it is necessary to establish a forcing sequence, to enable North to reveal his major suit distribution.

(2) ♠ K 10 4 2   ♡ A 5 3   ◇ K J 5   ♣ Q 10 7

Three notrump. New minor forcing would be an exercise in futility since it is clear that no eight card major suit fit exists. Don't trot out conventions that do not accomplish anything for your team.

(3) ♠ J 10 8 5 4   ♡ K 9 8 7   ◇ Q 5 4   ♣ 3

Two hearts. By not utilizing new minor forcing, partner is warned that responder is totally uninterested in game. Opener should pass or return to two spades.

(4) ♠ K J 9 8 4   ♡ J 3 2   ◇ Q 10 8 7   ♣ 8

Pass. This is a disadvantage of new minor forcing. Since two diamonds would be artificial, responder can't show a weak major-minor two suiter.

Opener's Rebids

New minor forcing is an attempt to elicit information about the precise shape of opener's hand. Thus:

(a) With three card support for responder's original major, opener rebids two of that major.

(b) With four cards in the unbid major, opener rebids two of that major.

(c) With both (a) and (b), opener rebids two of responder's major, planning to bid the other major later.*

(d) With none of the above, opener rebids two notrump or rebids his minor.

After the auction:

North	South
1 ♣	1 ♠
1 NT	2 ◇

how would you (North) best describe your distribution to partner on each of the following hands?

(1) ♠ A 3 2   ♡ K J 3   ◇ A 5   ♣ J 10 9 3 2

Two spades. This tells partner that you hold three card trump support, which must be valuable information if he happens to hold five or more spades.

(2) ♠ J 7   ♡ Q 5 3   ◇ A 5 4   ♣ A Q 9 7 6

Two notrump. With scattered values and no major suit fit, this bid best describes the hand.

---

*Alternatively, with both (a) and (b), opener can raise partner's artificial bid.

(3) ♠ K 4 ♡ 9 8 5 3 ◇ A 10 7 ♣ A K 9 8

Two hearts. Don't be afraid of the shabby quality of your heart suit. South might be looking at

♠ A Q 7 6 3 ♡ A K J 4 ◇ 3 ♣ Q 5 4

and he will be quite pleased to find out about your four card heart holding.

(4) ♠ A 5 4 ♡ K J 9 8 ◇ K 4 ♣ K 10 9 8

Two spades.* This bid shows a three card trump fit and says nothing about the four card heart suit. At your next turn, you may have a chance to clarify the situation. A possible auction:

North	South
1 ♣	1 ♠
1 NT	2 ◇
2 ♠	2 NT
3 ♡	

Now you've gotten the whole hand off your chest.

*Alternatively, three diamonds would show three spades and four hearts.

Here are some hands from actual play to illustrate new minor forcing.

(1)

North
♠ A Q 9 5 4
♡ A 8 7 4
◇ 5 4
♣ 7 3

South
♠ K 7
♡ K 9 6
◇ J 7 2
♣ A Q J 9 8

North	East	South	West
Pass	Pass	1 ♣	Pass
1 ♠	Pass	1 NT	Pass
2 ◇	Pass	3 ♣	Pass
Pass	Pass		

After South's one notrump rebid, North employed new minor forcing in an effort to find a major suit fit. If opener held either three spades or four hearts, North would have tried for game since his two minor suit doubletons would have added distributional values.

When South bid three clubs, North knew that no major suit fit existed and there was some reason not to play notrump. With all of these negatives in mind, he passed, settling for the part score.

Four spades is a reasonable contract dependent on either clubs behaving or a 3-3 spade break, but it is a hard contract to reach and is certainly not cold. Three rounds of diamonds forces declarer to ruff; a bad spade break would cost him control of the hand.

(2)

North
- ♠ A Q 7 5 4
- ♡ K 10 9 8
- ◊ Q 3
- ♣ Q 4

South
- ♠ K 10 8
- ♡ A 5
- ◊ 10 4 2
- ♣ A K 8 7 5

North	East	South	West
—	Pass	1 ♣	Pass
1 ♠	Pass	1 NT	Pass
2 ◊	Dbl	2 ♠	Pass
4 ♠	Pass	Pass	Pass

Despite East's lead directing double, South completes the description of his hand by showing three card spade support. (As it happens, East's double makes no difference on this hand, but a disadvantage of any artificial bid is the possibility of a lead directing double.)

The defense cashed two diamonds and led a third diamond. North ruffed, played the ace and king of trump, ruffed a heart and drew the final trumps. Now he claimed the balance of the tricks, discarding his losing heart on a high club.

Summary

"New minor forcing" is a useful tool to classify responder's rebid as invitational, game forcing, or weak. Artificial bids always give the opposition a chance to compete via lead directing doubles — this is a disadvantage of new minor forcing. However, weighing the pros and cons, you gain more than you lose in bidding accuracy.

To play new minor forcing effectively, a partnership must become aware of the possible inferences of all the various sequences. Some players feel that the amount of work involved just isn't worth it. Experiment and see if you like it. If you don't, you can survive effectively without it.

TOUT EST FACILE AVEC DE LA PATIENCE

This final section is devoted to a review of the material in this book. Needless to say, it is a series of bridge hands, but it is most emphatically not a pass-fail test! It is rather a section designed to help you become a successful five card majorite.

An auction coupled with four hands will be presented; your job will be to analyze the auction and find the correct bid for each of the hands.

With this format, you should be able to tighten up any weak spots. Thus, if a limit raise sequence causes you problems, it is easy to thumb back to the section on limit raises.

Good luck, and as the title of this section suggests,

EVERYTHING IS EASY WITH PATIENCE!

(1)	North	East	South	West
	1 ♠	Pass	2 ♠	Pass
	3 ◊*	Pass	?	

*Help suit game try

You hold:

(a) ♠ 7 5 3 2   ♡ K J 7 6   ◊ 4   ♣ Q 10 7 4

(b) ♠ J 6 4   ♡ J 8   ◊ A K J 4   ♣ 5 4 3 2

(c) ♠ 10 7 4   ♡ A K 10 3   ◊ 8 6 5   ♣ 9 8 4

(d) ♠ Q J 3 2   ♡ 7 3 2   ◊ 10 4   ♣ A 9 8 5

(2)	North	East	South	West
	1 ♠	Pass	2 ♡	Pass
	3 ♡	Pass	?	

You hold:

(a) ♠ J 3   ♡ A K J 5 4   ◊ Q 3 2   ♣ K 7 4

(b) ♠ A 7   ♡ K Q J 5 2   ◊ 10 9 7 6   ♣ K 3

(c) ♠ 3   ♡ Q 10 9 6 3 2   ◊ A Q   ♣ K 7 4 2

(d) ♠ J   ♡ K Q J 10 5 3   ◊ K Q   ♣ K J 10 4

(3)	North	East	South	West
	1 ♣	Pass	1 ♡	Pass
	2 ♡	Pass	2 ♠	Pass
	?			

You hold:

(a) ♠ J 6 2   ♡ A K 7 4   ◊ K 9 7   ♣ K 4 3

(b) ♠ 7   ♡ K 7 6 2   ◊ A Q 4   ♣ A 9 8 7 5

(c) ♠ A 5 4 2   ♡ K 7 6 4   ◊ 3   ♣ A Q 10 9

(d) ♠ Q 7 3   ♡ J 5 4 2   ◊ K Q 10   ♣ A Q 5

(4)	North	East	South	West
	1 ♣	Pass	1 ♠	Pass
	1 NT	Pass	2 ◊*	Pass
	?			

*New Minor Forcing

You hold:

(a) ♠ K 3 ♡ A 5 3 2 ◇ Q J 8 ♣ A 8 5 4

(b) ♠ A 10 9 ♡ K Q 10 ◇ J 3 2 ♣ K 10 3 2

(c) ♠ A 9 7 ♡ K 7 6 5 ◇ Q J 3 ♣ K 7 6

(d) ♠ 3 2 ♡ K J 6 ◇ K J 9 ♣ A Q 10 5 4

(5)	North	East	South	West
	2 ◇ *	Pass	2 NT	Pass
	?			

*Flannery

You hold:

(a) ♠ A Q 7 6 ♡ A J 10 7 4 ◇ K 6 2 ♣ 7

(b) ♠ K J 5 2 ♡ Q 10 7 4 2 ◇ K Q ♣ Q 2

(c) ♠ A K 10 7 ♡ A Q 10 9 8 ◇ 10 4 ♣ 9 8

(d) ♠ K Q J 3 ♡ J 10 7 6 4 ◇ A Q 4 2 ♣ —

(6)	North	East	South	West
	1 ♠	Dbl	2 ♠	?

You hold:

(a) ♠ J 7 ♡ K 3 2 ◇ Q J 7 6 ♣ Q 7 5 3

(b) ♠ J 7 3 2 ♡ A K 5 3 ◇ Q J 6 ♣ 7 5

(c) ♠ K Q 9 6 2 ♡ 3 ◇ A 5 4 2 ♣ 8 6 4

(d) ♠ — ♡ A K 7 6 ◇ A 9 8 7 ♣ J 10 9 7 4

(7)	North	East	South	West
	1 ♠	Pass	1 NT	Pass
	2 ♣	Pass	?	

You hold:

(a) ♠ Q 3 ♡ J 7 6 3 ◇ A 7 6 3 ♣ Q 10 7

(b) ♠ 7 ♡ K J 9 8 7 6 ◇ 8 4 3 ♣ K 10 9

(c) ♠ A 5 3 ♡ A 6 ◇ Q 10 8 4 ♣ 7 6 5 3

(d) ♠ 5 ♡ J 7 6 ◇ A 9 6 4 ♣ K J 10 9 7

(8)

North	East	South	West
1 ♣	Pass	1 ♠	Pass
1 NT	Pass	?	

You hold:

(a) ♠ A 10 3 2   ♡ K J 7   ◇ Q J 3   ♣ 10 9 3

(b) ♠ A 10 5 4 3   ♡ K 7 3   ◇ K 5 4   ♣ J 7

(c) ♠ J 5 4 3 2   ♡ A K J 8   ◇ K 3 2   ♣ Q

(d) ♠ A 9 8 4   ♡ A 3   ◇ J 9 8 7   ♣ J 7 4

(9)

North	East	South	West
1 ◇	1 ♠	Dbl	Pass
?			

You hold:

(a) ♠ K 9 8   ♡ A Q J 7   ◇ K Q 10 5 4   ♣ 3

(b) ♠ A Q 7   ♡ K 3 2   ◇ K 10 7 3 2   ♣ Q 2

(c) ♠ A Q 7   ♡ K 3 2   ◇ A K 5 4 2   ♣ K 8

(d) ♠ —   ♡ A Q 10 8   ◇ A J 10 7 6   ♣ A J 9 7

(10)

North	East	South	West
1 ♡	Pass	2 NT*	Pass
3 ◇	Pass	?	

*Jacoby 2 NT

You hold:

(a) ♠ A K 7   ♡ K 5 4 2   ◇ 10 7 3 2   ♣ K 2

(b) ♠ A Q 7   ♡ Q 10 9 8   ◇ K Q 10 2   ♣ J 4

(c) ♠ K Q   ♡ J 9 8 7   ◇ A 9 7   ♣ K Q 4 2

(d) ♠ K J 3   ♡ A K 5 4   ◇ J 7 4   ♣ Q 8 7

(11)

North	East	South	West
1 ♡	Pass	3 ♠ *	Pass
?			

*Splinter

You hold:

(a) ♠ K Q 8   ♡ A Q 9 7 5 2   ◊ K 5 3   ♣ 8

(b) ♠ A 9 8   ♡ A J 10 8 4   ◊ 7   ♣ A Q 8 7

(c) ♠ Q 10 7   ♡ A K 10 5 4   ◊ A Q   ♣ K 5 4

(d) ♠ K Q 10   ♡ Q 10 9 8 7   ◊ K Q 10   ♣ K 8

ANSWERS

(1)

North	East	South	West
1 ♠	Pass	2 ♠	Pass
3 ◇ *	Pass	?	

*Help suit game try

(a)   ♠ 7 5 3 2   ♡ K J 7 6   ◇ 4   ♣ Q 10 7 4

Four spades. Partner is asking for help in the diamond suit and your singleton diamond is just what the doctor ordered. He should be able to ruff away his potential diamond losers, making four spades a pianola.

(b)   ♠ J 6 4   ♡ J 8   ◇ A K J 4   ♣ 5 4 3 2

Four spades. This time your help is in high cards, but the effect is the same. Partner was worried about diamond losers and you have him covered.

(c)   ♠ 10 7 4   ♡ A K 10 3   ◇ 8 6 5   ♣ 9 8 4

Three spades. If partner needs diamond help, you have the worst possible holding. Let him know this by declining the game try.

(d)   ♠ Q J 3 2   ♡ 7 3 2   ◇ 10 4   ♣ A 9 8 5

Three spades. A very close decision. With a doubleton in partner's game try suit, check the general strength of your hand. Since this hand is of minimum quality for the two spade raise, declining the game try will more often than not prove to be the winning action.

(2)	North	East	South	West
	1 ♠	Pass	2 ♡	Pass
	3 ♡	Pass	?	

(a) ♠ J 3   ♡ A K J 5 4   ◊ Q 3 2   ♣ K 7 4

Four hearts. Although opener is showing a healthy opening by bidding three hearts instead of four hearts, you have nothing to offer beyond your original two heart response. Any further moves must be left to partner.

(b) ♠ A 7   ♡ K Q J 5 2   ◊ 10 9 7 6   ♣ K 3

Three spades. Inaugurating a mild slam try. The solidity of your hearts plus the possibility of runnable spades make slam a real possibility. If opener bids four clubs, retreat to four hearts. You've made your move; the rest is up to him. However, if he cuebids diamonds, things get much more interesting. Your next move then would be four notrump, asking for more information. (It would not be Blackwood in this sequence, since once you start a cuebidding sequence, Blackwood is no longer used.)

(c) ♠ 3   ♡ Q 10 9 6 3 2   ◊ A Q   ♣ K 7 4 2

Four hearts. There are simply too many holes in this hand for slam unless opener bids again.

(d) ♠ J   ♡ K Q J 10 5 3   ◊ K Q   ♣ K J 10 7

Four notrump. With this whale of a hand, all you care about is aces. It is unlikely that the five level will be in jeopardy since opener is a prohibitive favorite to hold at least two aces.

(3)	North	East	South	West
	1 ♣	Pass	1 ♡	Pass
	2 ♡	Pass	2 ♠	Pass
	?			

(a) ♠ J 6 2   ♡ A K 7 4   ◊ K 9 7   ♣ K 4 3

Three hearts. You are not quite sure if partner is making a help suit game try, looking for notrump, or moving towards slam, but it really doesn't matter. Your job is to show a minimum hand with little help in spades.

(b) ♠ 7 ♡ K 7 6 2 ◇ A Q 4 ♣ A 9 8 7 5

Four hearts. In the light of partner's two spade bid, your hand should be an excellent dummy with hearts as trump. The singleton spade is a terrific asset.

(c) ♠ A 5 4 2 ♡ K 7 6 4 ◇ 3 ♣ A Q 10 9

Three spades. Since you intend to accept any game try, complete the description of your hand by raising spades. Partner should work out that you have a shortage in diamonds and can act accordingly.

(d) ♠ Q 7 3 ♡ J 5 4 2 ◇ K Q 10 ♣ A Q 5

Two notrump. Despite the fact that you hold four hearts, the flatness of this hand plus double stoppers in the minors may make the nine trick notrump game easier than the ten trick heart game. (If partner's spade bid is a cue bid, he should correct to hearts.)

(4)

North	East	South	West
1 ♣	Pass	1 ♠	Pass
1 NT	Pass	2 ◇*	Pass
?			

*New Minor Forcing

(a) ♠ K 3 ♡ A 5 3 2 ◇ Q J 8 ♣ A 8 5 4

Two hearts. Partner is asking for clarification of your major suit holding.

(b) ♠ A 10 9 ♡ K Q 10 ◇ J 3 2 ♣ K 10 3 2

Two spades. This bid shows three spades and, according to the methods advocated in this book, denies four hearts.

(c) ♠ A 9 7 ♡ K 7 6 5 ◇ Q J 3 ♣ K 7 6

Three diamonds. This shows both three card spade support and four hearts. Some experts prefer to bid spades, planning to introduce hearts later, but we believe this can lead to ambiguous auctions. There is little danger of three diamonds getting the contract too high. The new minor forcing must be of at least invitational strength and a fit for whichever major partner prefers must be a plus factor.

(d)   ♠ 3 2   ♡ K J 6   ◇ K J 9   ♣ A Q 10 5 4

Three notrump. When notrump is bid after new minor forcing, it denies both three card support of partner's suit and four of the other major. Partner may hold only invitational rather than game forcing values and two notrump may be passed; with this maximum notrump rebid, make sure you reach game.

(5) | North | East | South | West |
|---|---|---|---|
| 2 ◇* | Pass | 2 NT | Pass |
| ? | | | |

*Flannery

(a)   ♠ A Q 7 6   ♡ A J 10 7 4   ◇ K 6 2   ♣ 7

Three diamonds. Two notrump asks for clarification of your opening bid. Your bid shows three diamonds and a singleton club.

(b)   ♠ K J 5 2   ♡ Q 10 7 4 2   ◇ K Q   ♣ Q 2

Three hearts. Over two notrump a bid of either major shows 4-5-2-2 distribution with hearts as a minimum and spades as a maximum. With thirteen high card points, major suit concentration and controls are the critical factors. Treat this hand as a minimum range Flannery opening.

(c)   ♠ A K 10 7   ♡ A Q 10 9 8   ◇ 10 4   ♣ 9 8

Three spades. Compare this thirteen high card point hand to the previous example. Here, all your high cards are "working," since they are concentrated in the majors. Your three spade rebid signals this encouraging fact.

(d)   ♠ K Q J 3   ♡ J 10 7 6 4   ◇ A Q 4 2   ♣ —

Four diamonds. The correct Flannery rebid to show a four card diamond suit. Partner will know you are void in clubs, a fact which will no doubt be very helpful in the decision making process.

(6)	North	East	South	West
1 ♠	Dbl	2 ♠	?

(a)   ♠ J 7   ♡ K 3 2   ◊ Q J 7 6   ♣ Q 7 5 3

Double. This is a responsive double, showing the desire to compete but denying four hearts. The responsive double solves this very awkward situation. Without responsive doubles, this is an extremely difficult hand to describe.

(b)   ♠ J 7 3 2   ♡ A K 5 3   ◊ Q J 6   ♣ 7 5

Four hearts. Partner should have four hearts for his takeout double and with this many high card points, game should be tried. Even if partner doubled on subminimum values, game should have some chance of success, since he undoubtedly is short in spades.

(c)   ♠ K Q 9 6 2   ♡ 3   ◊ A 5 4 2   ♣ 8 6 4

Pass. If you weren't playing responsive doubles, you would gleefully double for penalties. As it is, you must pass and hope the auction doesn't die.

(d)   ♠ —   ♡ A K 7 6   ◊ A 9 8 7   ♣ J 10 9 7 4

Three spades. With a hand this good, the opponents must be bidding on a wing and a prayer. You are liable to run into a barrage of spade preempts, but you should be thinking slam and not sell out under the five level.

(7)	North	East	South	West
1 ♠	Pass	1 NT	Pass
2 ♣	Pass	?

(a)   ♠ Q 3   ♡ J 7 6 3   ◊ A 7 6 3   ♣ Q 10 7

Two spades. Do not even consider passing two clubs; opener may hold a three card club suit and will not be overjoyed at the prospect of a 3-3 fit. Opt for the sure 5-2 fit. You are not nearly strong enough for two notrump.

(b)   ♠ 7   ♡ K J 9 8 7 6   ◊ 8 4 3   ♣ K 10 9

Two hearts. Opener will know that you hold a long heart suit with insufficient strength for an immediate two over one bid. The forcing notrump allows this type of auction.

178

(c) ♠ A 5 3   ♡ A 6   ◇ Q 10 8 4   ♣ 7 6 5 3

Three spades, continuing the plan of your original forcing notrump response. This bid shows a hand of limit raise strength containing only three trumps.

(d) ♠ 5   ♡ J 7 6   ◇ A 9 6 4   ♣ K J 10 9 7

Three clubs. Your hand has improved by virtue of partner's rebid. You are assured of an eight card fit even if opener has only three clubs. With a good hand, opener will bid again. If he passes, you are probably in the right spot.

(8) | North | East | South | West |
|---|---|---|---|
| 1 ♣ | Pass | 1 ♠ | Pass |
| 1 NT | Pass | ? | |

(a) ♠ A 10 3 2   ♡ K J 7   ◇ Q J 3   ♣ 10 9 3

Two notrump. There is no eight card major suit fit, so invite opener to carry on to game with a maximum one notrump rebid. If opener passes two notrump, you've done your job.

(b) ♠ A 10 5 4 3   ♡ K 7 3   ◇ K 5 4   ♣ J 7

Two diamonds. Employ new minor forcing to find out more about opener's hand. If he bids two spades, invite with three spades. After a two heart response, bid two notrump and leave the final decision to partner.

(c) ♠ J 5 4 3 2   ♡ A K J 8   ◇ K 3 2   ♣ Q

Two diamonds. You certainly have enough power for game; the only question is where. If partner shows spade support or a four card heart suit, bid game in the major. If he shows both majors, choose hearts as your resting place; a 4-4 heart fit rates to be better than a 5-3 spade fit. If partner shows neither major, bid three notrump.

(d) ♠ A 9 8 4   ♡ A 3   ◇ J 9 8 7   ♣ J 7 4

Pass. You simply don't have enough to invite game. One notrump should be a safe enough contract. Don't look for trouble.

(9)	North	East	South	West
	1 ◇	1 ♠	Dbl	Pass
	?			

(a) ♠ K 9 8 ♡ A Q J 7 ◇ K Q 10 5 4 ♣ 3

Three hearts. Partner's negative double promises at least four hearts. With a proven trump fit, your singleton club has added materially to your playing strength.

(b) ♠ A Q 7 ♡ K 3 2 ◇ K 10 7 3 2 ♣ Q 2

One notrump. This describes a minimum opening bid with spades well stopped, which is exactly what you have.

(c) ♠ A Q 7 ♡ K 3 2 ◇ A K 5 4 2 ♣ K 8

Two notrump. Since you intended to rebid two notrump without the overcall, there is no reason not to do so anyway. The spade overcall should cause no anxiety since you hold a double spade stopper.

(d) ♠ — ♡ A Q 10 8 ◇ A J 10 7 6 ♣ A J 9 7

Two spades. What started out as a good hand has become a giant as a result of the auction. Get this across to partner by a game forcing cue bid.

(10)	North	East	South	West
	1 ♡	Pass	2 NT*	Pass
	3 ◇	Pass	?	

*Jacoby 2 NT

(a) ♠ A K 7 ♡ K 5 4 2 ◇ 10 7 3 2 ♣ K 2

Three spades. Opener has announced a singleton diamond. Your lack of wasted diamond honors is an encouraging sign. Tell this to partner by cuebidding your ace of spades.

(b) ♠ A Q 7 ♡ Q 10 9 8 ◇ K Q 10 2 ♣ J 4

Four hearts. This is the reverse of the previous hand because your diamond holding is duplicated by partner's singleton. Discourage partner's slam aspirations by leaping to four hearts.

(c)   ♠ K Q   ♡ J 9 8 7   ◇ A 9 7   ♣ K Q 4 2

Four diamonds. Lack of duplication is a definite plus factor. Four diamonds is, of course, a cuebid. Opener should know that you are interested in bigger and better things, but have no side ace other than the ace of diamonds.

(d)   ♠ K J 3   ♡ A K 5 4   ◇ J 7 4   ♣ Q 8 7

Three hearts. You have nothing to cuebid but also you have no diamond duplication. By bidding three hearts, you provide partner with room to explore if he wishes to do so.

(11) | North | East | South | West |
|-------|------|-------|------|
| 1 ♡ | Pass | 3 ♠ * | Pass |
| ? | | | |

*Splinter

(a)   ♠ K Q 8   ♡ A Q 9 7 5 2   ◇ K 5 3   ♣ 8

Four hearts. Spade duplication makes slam an unlikely bet. Partner will know this when you decline further exploration.

(b)   ♠ A 9 8   ♡ A J 10 8 4   ◇ 7   ♣ A Q 8 7

Four clubs. You have an excellent opening bid which has been improved by the auction. If partner signs off with four hearts, make another try by cuebidding the ace of spades.

(c)   ♠ Q 10 7   ♡ A K 10 5 4   ◇ A Q   ♣ K 5 4

Four notrump. You have a good opening bid outside of the splinter suit, plus good controls. Slam is very likely unless partner has bid on nothing.

(d)   ♠ K Q 10   ♡ Q 10 9 8 7   ◇ K Q 10   ♣ K 8

Three notrump. This bid conveys your firm double stopper in spades opposite partner's singleton. Although he is likely to correct to four hearts, this bid gives him an opportunity to either pass or cuebid, armed with the knowledge of extreme duplication. He should also work out that you have at least a very healthy minimum, else you would have signed off in four hearts.

Andersen THE LEBENSOHL CONVENTION COMPLETE	$ 6.95
Baron THE BRIDGE PLAYER'S DICTIONARY	$19.95
Bergen BETTER BIDDING WITH BERGEN, Vol. I, Uncontested Auctions	$11.95
Bergen BETTER BIDDING WITH BERGEN, Vol. II, Competitive Auctions	$ 9.95
Blackwood COMPLETE BOOK OF OPENING LEADS	$17.95
Blackwood-Hanson PLAY FUNDAMENTALS	$ 6.95
Boeder THINKING ABOUT IMPS	$12.95
Bruno-Hardy 2 OVER 1 GAME FORCE: AN INTRODUCTION	$ 9.95
Darvas & De V. Hart RIGHT THROUGH THE PACK	$14.95
DeSerpa THE MEXICAN CONTRACT	$ 5.95
Eber & Freeman HAVE I GOT A STORY FOR YOU	$ 7.95
Feldheim FIVE CARD MAJOR BIDDING IN CONTRACT BRIDGE	$12.95
Flannery THE FLANNERY 2 DIAMOND OPENING	$ 7.95
Goldman ACES SCIENTIFIC	$ 9.95
Goldman WINNERS AND LOSERS AT THE BRIDGE TABLE	$ 3.95
Groner DUPLICATE BRIDGE DIRECTION	$14.95
Hardy	
COMPETITIVE BIDDING WITH 2-SUITED HANDS	$ 9.95
TWO-OVER-ONE GAME FORCE	$14.95
TWO-OVER-ONE GAME FORCE QUIZ BOOK	$11.95
Harris BRIDGE DIRECTOR'S COMPANION (3rd Edition)	$19.95
Kay COMPLETE BOOK OF DUPLICATE BRIDGE	$14.95
Kearse BRIDGE CONVENTIONS COMPLETE	$29.95
Kelsey THE TRICKY GAME	$11.95
Lampert THE FUN WAY TO ADVANCED BRIDGE	$11.95
Lawrence	
CARD COMBINATIONS	$12.95
COMPLETE BOOK ON BALANCING	$11.95
COMPLETE BOOK ON OVERCALLS	$11.95
DYNAMIC DEFENSE	$11.95
FALSECARDS	$ 9.95
HAND EVALUATION	$11.95
HOW TO READ YOUR OPPONENTS' CARDS	$11.95
JUDGMENT AT BRIDGE	$ 9.95
PARTNERSHIP UNDERSTANDINGS	$ 5.95
PLAY BRIDGE WITH MIKE LAWRENCE	$11.95
PLAY SWISS TEAMS WITH MIKE LAWRENCE	$ 9.95
WORKBOOK ON THE TWO OVER ONE SYSTEM	$11.95

Lawrence & Hanson WINNING BRIDGE INTANGIBLES ....$ 4.95
Lipkin INVITATION TO ANNIHILATION ....$ 8.95
Michaels & Cohen 4-3-2-1 MANUAL ....$ 4.95
Penick BEGINNING BRIDGE COMPLETE ....$ 9.95
Penick BEGINNING BRIDGE QUIZZES ....$ 6.95
Robinson WASHINGTON STANDARD $19.95
Rosenkranz
    BRIDGE: THE BIDDER'S GAME $12.95
    TIPS FOR TOPS ....$ 9.95
    MORE TIPS FOR TOPS ....$ 9.95
    TRUMP LEADS ....$ 7.95
    OUR MAN GODFREY $10.95
Rosenkranz & Alder BID TO WIN, PLAY FOR PLEASURE $11.95
Rosenkranz & Truscott BIDDING ON TARGET $10.95
Silverman
    ELEMENTARY BRIDGE FIVE CARD MAJOR STUDENT TEXT ....$ 4.95
    INTERMEDIATE BRIDGE FIVE CARD MAJOR STUDENT TEXT ....$ 4.95
    ADVANCED & DUPLICATE BRIDGE STUDENT TEXT ....$ 4.95
    PLAY OF THE HAND AS DECLARER
      & DEFENDER STUDENT TEXT ....$ 4.95
Simon
    CUT FOR PARTNERS ....$ 9.95
    WHY YOU LOSE AT BRIDGE $11.95
Stewart & Baron
    THE BRIDGE BOOK, Vol. 1, Beginning ....$ 9.95
    THE BRIDGE BOOK, Vol. 2, Intermediate ....$ 9.95
    THE BRIDGE BOOK, Vol. 3, Advanced ....$ 9.95
    THE BRIDGE BOOK, Vol. 4, Defense ....$ 7.95
Truscott BID BETTER, PLAY BETTER $12.95
Von Elsner
    EVERYTHING'S JAKE WITH ME ....$ 5.95
    THE BEST OF JAKE WINKMAN ....$ 5.95
Wei PRECISION BIDDING SYSTEM ....$ 7.95
Woolsey
    MATCHPOINTS $14.95
    MODERN DEFENSIVE SIGNALLING ....$ 4.95
    PARTNERSHIP DEFENSE $12.95
World Bridge Federation APPEALS COMMITTEE DECISIONS
    from the 1994 NEC WORLD CHAMPIONSHIPS ....$ 9.95